MESSENGER OF MORTALITY

EDITED AND DESIGNED BY
JULIAN ROTHENSTEIN

REDSTONE PRESS
IN ASSOCIATION WITH THE SOUTH BANK CENTRE

For Hiang Kee, Lucien and Ella.

First Published in 1989
by Redstone Press,
7a St Lawrence Terrace,
London W10 5SU, England

in association with the South Bank Centre

Introduction © Peter Wollen 1989

EDITOR'S ACKNOWLEDGEMENTS

Many thanks to Peter Wollen for his introduction, and to Jo Labanyi of the Department of Spanish, University College London, who translated the headlines and humorous verses. Thanks also to Roger Malbert and Fernando Leal Audirac who checked the proofs and had many good ideas. I am grateful to Michael Rothenstein who introduced me to Posada, The Canning House Library, Isabella McEwen, Christabel Gurney who typeset the book, Joanna Drew, Tania Butler, Liz Allen of the South Bank Centre for their support and to Nina Kidron who gave me much useful advice about the book's production.   J.R.

Grateful acknowledgement is made to The Elephant Trust for their grant.

'José Guadalupe Posada: Printmaker to the Mexican People,' and 'Posada's Dance of Death,' from *An Artist on Art, Collected Essays of Jean Charlot, Volume II, Mexican Art,* published in 1972 are reprinted with kind permission from The University of Hawaii Press.

'José Guadalupe Posada' by Diego Rivera in *Arte y Politica* is reprinted with kind permission from Editorial Grijalbo, S.A.

Typeset by Wayzgoose Phototypesetting.
Printed and Bound in England by Woolnough Bookbinding Ltd.

British Library Cataloguing in Publication Data
Posada, J.G. 1852-1913
    Messenger of mortality
    1. Mexican engravings, Posada, J.G., 1852-1913
    2. Title II. Rothenstein, Julian, 1948-
III. South Bank Centre
769.92.4
ISBN 1-870003-45-4
ISBN 1-870003-15-2

Posada and his son, about 1900

CONTENTS

Introduction PETER WOLLEN 14

Calavera of the People's Printer 24

Chronology JULIA ENGELHARDT 26

THE PRINTS

DEMONS AND VIRGINS 31

LOVE 55

COMETS AND DISASTERS 67

DON CHEPITO MARIHUANO 78

PRIVATE CONFLICTS AND SUICIDES 81

POLITICS AND NATIONAL EVENTS 99

RARE CASES 117

CALAVERAS 123

BATTLES, MURDERS AND ASSASSINATIONS 149

COMMERCIAL ART 163

Page from *Minotaure No. 10* ANDRÉ BRETON 172

Printmaker to the Mexican People JEAN CHARLOT 173

Posada's Dance of Death JEAN CHARLOT 178

Four Calaveras by MANUEL MANILLA 183

José Guadalupe Posada DIEGO RIVERA 185

Bibliography 187

TRANSLATIONS FROM THE SPANISH BY JO LABANYI

PRINTING SHOP
OF A. VANEGAS ARROYO
founded in the nineteenth century in 1880

In this long-established firm will be found a varied and select assortment
of songs for the current year, collections of congratulations, magic tricks,
riddles, parlour games, booklets on cooking, candy-making and
pastry-making, toasts, rhymes for clowns, patriotic speeches, plays for
children or puppets, charming stories;

THE NEW ORACLE, or THE BOOK OF THE FUTURE;
RULES FOR TELLING FORTUNES WITH CARDS;
THE NEW MEXICAN FORTUNE-TELLER;
BLACK AND WHITE MAGIC,
or THE BOOK OF SORCERERS.

IMPRENTA
DE A. VANEGAS ARROYO
(fundada en el Siglo XIX año de 1880)

En esta antigua casa se halla un variado y selecto surtido de canciones para el presente año.

Coleccion de Felicitaciones, Suertes de Prestidigitacion, Adivinanzas, Juegos de Estrado, Cuadernos de Cocina, Dulcero, Pastelero, Brindis, Versos para Payaso, Discursos Patrióticos, Comedias para niños é titeres Bonitos Cuentos.

→ EL NUEVO ORÁCULO ←

O SEA EL LIBRO DEL PORVENIR
Reglas para echar las cartas.

— EL NUEVO AGORERO MEXICANO —

LA MAGIA PRIETA Y BLANCA
O sea el libro de los Brujos.

INTRODUCTION

PETER WOLLEN

JOSÉ GUADALUPE POSADA died in 1913, soon after the beginning of the Mexican Revolution. Although he had spent a prolific life as an engraver and etcher, working mainly for the penny press, he was not well-known or widely acclaimed. In fact, he was buried in a pauper's grave by neighbours only one of whom was literate.[1] Even today very little is known about his life. His rise to fame, the growth of the Posada legend, is due to the generation of artists who changed the direction of Mexican art in the years after the Revolution. The painter Dr Atl, the most persistent early pioneer of modernism in Mexico, and the young French immigrant, Jean Charlot, one of the group of muralists around Diego Rivera, were the first to notice Posada's work in the new artistic context of the post-revolutionary years.[2] Charlot, who saw his first Posada prints in 1920, followed up his discovery, showed prints to other painters and wrote the first biographical and critical essays on Posada's work, in the early twenties. In time, other artists — including Rivera, José Clemente Orozco and David Alfaro Siqueiros — took up Posada's cause, often in hyperbolic terms, and acknowledged their debt, direct or indirect, to the humble popular print-maker. The legend was born.[3]

Now that Posada is respected, studied, collected and exhibited, we are aware of the breadth and range of his work. But his entry into art history was due especially to the more lurid prints that he made for the small press owner and publisher, Antonio Vanegas Arroyo, who employed Posada to illustrate the topical ballads and sensational *canards* he wrote and hawked around the streets and at fairs, pilgrimages and public gatherings. Above all, it was the *calaveras*, vivid and lively skeletons and skulls with grinning teeth, dancing, cycling, playing the guitar, plying their trades, drinking, masquerading, which seized the imagination of artists and writers. The *calaveras* were produced to be sold on the 2nd of November, the Mexican Day of the Dead, eye-catching skeletons, accompanied by jocular and satirical verses, designed to entertain and enliven the festivities.

Originally, the demand for Posada prints came 'from below', from the poor and the illiterate. The new appreciation of them 'from above' formed part of a much wider discovery and re-evaluation of Mexican popular art and imagery of many different kinds. Posada prints took their place alongside such other forms as *pulquería* paintings, the fantastic scenes painted on the walls of cheap dives selling *pulque* and other kinds of grog and rotgut, rather like inn-signs, and *retablos*, the ex-voto paintings, usually on tin, which were nailed upon church walls to commemorate some miraculous recovery from disaster or escape from near death, due to the invocation of a favourite saint, vividly portraying the catastrophe in question and the rescue from it, in a kind of comic-strip-cum-naive style. Posada's etchings and engravings seemed in the same register, showed the same startling directness, grim humour and unpredictable imagination.

Moreover, in Posada's case, a crucial connection can be discerned between the *calaveras* and the art of the pre-Columbian period, with its own profusion of skulls and pressing reminders of death. Indeed, the roots of the Day of the Dead were customarily traced back beyond their explicit origin in Spanish Catholicism to an older, implicit connection with the ancient Indian cults of human sacrifice and bloodletting, with their grisly furniture of skull racks and bloody obsidian knives.[4] It may seem a far cry from the top-hatted cyclist or skirt-hitching fandango dancer of Posada's *calavera* to the cruel grandeur of the pre-Columbian priesthood and its rites, but Posada's tiny storefront workshop at No. 5 Santa Ines Street (now *calle de la Moneda*) was, after all, only a stone's throw from the site of the great Aztec temple pyramid of Tenochtitlan.[5]

The artists of the Mexican renaissance were in full revolt against a tradition of dependence on European, especially Spanish, academic art. They wanted to replace it with an art whose genealogy would go back before the Conquest, which would be original to Mexico, popular and authentic. Partly, of course, as with other nationalist and revolutionary movements, this led to a revival of interest in folk art, in Indian toys, costume and pottery, the traditional arts of the village. But it also extended to the urban vernacular art of Posada. Posada was a trained draughtsman and print-maker (he attended the municipal trade school in his native town of Aguascalientes) and an unabashed commercial artist, seeking employment wherever he could find it and carrying out the commissions offered him by editors and publishers. But, in some ways, this made him closer to the fine artists and avant-gardists who admired his work — they, too, were trained and working to order, though from a very different background and with very different aesthetic values and ambitions. Posada formed a link between the folk tradition and the art of the muralists.

Indeed, muralism was a particular mode of 'street art', which could be compared with popular print-making. Many, though not all, of Rivera's murals were painted on exterior walls, designed to be seen and looked at by passers-by busy on some other business, not art-lovers, private owners or museum visitors. Muralism was presented and defended as a public form. Catchpenny prints and broadsheets, Posada's works were public too, though in a different way. Their place was the street, where they were hawked and sold by pedlars to a popular and often illiterate audience. They were not collected or exhibited in galleries. They illustrated *corridos*, ballads and verses, just as murals decorated buildings, both outside the confines of pure art. Like Rivera's murals, they often had topical themes and competed for attention with striking images and compositions, seeking to please an unsophisticated public.

The muralists themselves turned their hands to print-making, following the impetus given by Charlot's rediscovery of Posada. After the SYNDICATE OF REVOLUTIONARY PAINTERS, SCULPTORS AND ENGRAVERS OF MEXICO was founded in 1922, it published a magazine, *El Machete*, which was modelled on the old penny press, with more woodcuts and illustrations than text, many of them illustrating *corridos* and verse lampoons. Siqueiros and Xavier Guerrero were the most prolific contributors, although *El Machete* also carried work by Rivera and Orozco. (Orozco had himself begun his career as a cartoonist, for the well-known magazine *Ahuizote*, so that he had a much more direct link with the world of Posada than the other artists).[6] *El Machete* was, of course, an agitational vehicle, highly politicized in its content and Posada, too, was often presented, retrospectively, as a 'political artist', although in fact political topics are relatively rare in his output and he was capable of doing both pro-Díaz and anti-Díaz, pro-Madero and anti-Madero cartoons, presumably according to the political preference of his employers.

Today we can see how the post-Revolutionary artists, in their choice of muralism as a form and in their enthusiasm for Posada, reflected an extreme 'phase two' version of modernism, which rejected not only academic and figurative painting, but easel painting as a genre. The denunciation of easel painting was at its strongest in the Soviet Union, in the writings of Tarabukhin and Arvatov, and in the manifestos and propaganda of the Constructivist movement. Although this aesthetic developed separately in Mexico there were, of course, close ties between the two countries, and the left wing of Mexican artists looked to Soviet artists for an example. Rivera had been a member of a largely Russian exile milieu when he was in Paris and maintained his contacts after he left. Indeed, when he visited the Soviet Union in 1928 he signed the founding declaration of the October group of artists, which brought together architects, muralists, poster designers, book illustrators and cartoonists, on an explicit platform of 'public art' (implying the end of easel painting).

In fact, in some respects, Posada was more like Rivera and the others than they might have imagined. He was not a native intuitive genius, but a trained artist who altered and adapted his style to accommodate his public. If we look at Posada's early work we can see the influence of European engravers and print artists (such as Cham or Grandville). His prints are detailed, finished and technically sophisticated. It is only later that he simplifies his style, producing work which is much cruder but often more striking. In much the same way, Rivera simplified his work, abandoning both his *beaux arts* training and the highly sophisticated speculation and composition of his Cubist period, to produce images which many have thought crude and too fluently figurative, with a popular audience in mind. For Posada, the motive force ultimately was commercial, whereas for Rivera it was political, but the trajectories were similar.

Posada was far from being an amateur, like the *Douanier* Rousseau, to whom he has sometimes been compared.[7] Nor was he an anonymous professional — he signed his work, unlike many other print-makers (though not all of it). It was the signature, of course, which first enabled Charlot to find out more about him and categorize prints under his name. His workshop, round the corner from the art school of San Carlos, which both Rivera and Orozco attended at different times, also became part of the Posada legend. Both of them describe frequenting Posada's shop while they were at art school, thus enabling them to cast Posada not simply in the role of hero or precursor, but also teacher. Both claimed a direct contact (probably true for Orozco, but false for Rivera, at least according to Charlot — and Rivera, of course, was notorious as a fabulator and mythomane!).

In this sense, it is wrong to see Posada simply as an 'influence'. His name and legend were constitutive in the establishment of the Mexican renaissance; they symbolized both an alternative tradition and, crucially, a chain of succession. This particular role assigned to Posada was important both in relation to Mexicanism and in relation to Modernism. It gave credibility to claims to be part of an authentically

Mexican artistic tradition, crossing both the class gap and the historic divide of the Revolution itself and, at the same time, guaranteed the modernity of the tradition by aligning it with the revival of interest in popular imagery among the European avant-garde. It was a way of solving the classic dilemma of revolutionary nationalism — how to be popular, authentic, traditional *and* modernizing, all at the same time.

The European avant-garde had been interested in popular imagery at least since the time of the art critic and historian, Champfleury, and his friend, the painter Gustave Courbet. Champfleury's HISTOIRE DE L'IMAGERIE POPULAIRE was published in 1869 (though he had first written about popular prints long before, in 1850). Courbet's paintings, of course, date from the same period — 'The Meeting', painted in 1854, derives from a popular print of the Wandering Jew, which Champfleury also used as the frontispiece for his book.[8] The next wave of interest in prints was dominated by the newly discovered Japanese prints which decisively influenced the early phase of Modernism, though it was perhaps their exotic rather than their popular qualities which were significant for the artists concerned. A third wave comes after the beginning of Cubism — which brought with it yet another re-evaluation of non-canonical and 'primitive' forms of art. It is especially worth noting also the use of Russian *lubki* (broadsheets and chapbooks) made by the Golden Fleece and Donkey's Tail artists, especially Mikhail Larionov, Natalia Goncharova and, a little later, Kasimir Malevich.[9]

Larionov was also a collector of popular prints, including examples of the French *images d'Epinal* and Japanese woodcuts, as well as the Russian *lubok*, which were exhibited at a large exhibition of popular imagery that he organized, with Goncharova, in April 1913. Larionov was also a friend of Rivera and a frequent visitor to his studio, while they were both in Paris. In general, Rivera was well-informed on Russian popular art, due to the exhibition which Nathalie Ehrenburg, another friend, organized for the *salon d'automne* in the autumn of 1913 (where Rivera showed his early Cubist paintings). Indeed, it has been argued, by Ramón Favela, that it was these Russian influences that first induced Rivera to introduce Mexican motifs, such as *serape* stripes, into his Cubist work.[10] Certainly too, they prepared the ground for his immediate enthusiasm for Posada's work when it was shown to him by Charlot on his return to Mexico. In many ways Rivera saw the Mexican revolution, and Mexican post-revolutionary art, through the lens of the Russian revolution and Russian art.

In the Soviet Union, however, artists who had been influenced by the *lubki*, such as El Lissitsky or Vladimir Tatlin, moved away from them stylistically towards a much more abstract visual style or else, pulling in the opposite direction, towards the use of photography as a print medium, rather than woodcut or engraving. Evidently, this reflects the much greater impetus of a 'machine' aesthetic in the Soviet Union than in Mexico, as well as the demand for a 'protelarian' rather than a 'popular' art. Although there are some parallels with work like that of the *El Machete* artists, such as Vladimir Mayakovsky's 'Rosta windows', most Soviet artists, even though working with posters, broadsheets or illustrated books, moved away from the imagery of the *lubok.* Mexican artists stayed much closer to the folk tradition, to *Mexicanidad*, and this ensured the survival and reputation of an artist such as Posada. While artistic 'populism' came relatively late to Mexico, it grew deeper roots and lasted longer.

It could even be argued that the posthumous fame bestowed on Posada reflects the problematic path followed by the artists of the Mexican renaissance as they entered the 1930s. Whatever they may have said in their political rhetoric, they all of them, including Siqueiros, the most Stalinist, rejected 'Socialist Realism' stylistically in their painting. The origins of their art lay in their rejection of *beaux arts* academicism in the years of the *Porfiriato* and it was impossible for them to renege on this. On the other hand, their political commitments, the populist culture they had brought into being in the post revolutionary years, had entailed a rejection of abstract art and, indeed, 'difficult' minority-oriented avant-gardism in general. They tried to find a third path, both Modernist and figurative, without being avant-garde or academic (or academic-revivalist like socialist realism). In this context populism, a respect for the non-academic (because untrained) figurative forms of folk art, and especially of an 'urban' popular artist such as Posada, was intrinsic to their whole political and aesthetic strategy.

The Mexican artists set out to create an 'original' and independently Mexican version of Modernism and it is in this context that Posada has to be seen. Their interest in popular imagery is both a part of the broader discovery of 'low' and marginal art forms by modernists and at the same time a specific re-working of Modernism, which in turn entailed a specific attitude towards an artist such as Posada. The relationship between Mexican and European Modernism was complex, delicate and fraught with danger. There is no doubt that without the influence of Cubism and Russian avant-gardism, Posada would never have been recognized and praised in the way that he was. On the other hand, Posada also stood in a different relationship to the artists of the Mexican renaissance than the artists of the *lubok* did to Larionov or Vassily Kandinsky, or the artists of the German *moritaten* to George Grosz or Otto Dix. Posada was seen not just in terms of fresh material which could be purloined for new forms or imagery, or even as a repository of popular wisdom and insight in an unspoiled form, necessary for the rejuvenation or even completion of art, but as an artist in his own right, a beacon, an emblematic figure who pointed the way towards a specifically Mexican Modernism.

We can see the tensions clearly in the 1930s when Surrealism began to be known in Mexico. In due course, Rivera, who had begun as a Bukharinite, began to align himself with Trotsky, and thus draw closer to the Surrealists, who had already aligned themselves with Trotsky, as early as 1929. This re-alignment reached its culmination when André Breton himself came to Mexico in 1938, though it broke apart very soon afterwards. In 1937 Breton had given a lecture on 'black humour' at the Paris *exposition universelle* of that year and, when he was introduced to Posada, he immediately saw his work as exemplifying 'black humour' in an unmistakable way. On his return to Paris he set about compiling an anthology of 'black humour', which he completed in 1940, though publication was prohibited by the Vichy regime. Mexico became a privileged place for Breton, a surrealist country *par excellence* and Posada its exponent of 'black humour'. For the first time, the Posada who had been discovered by a Frenchman (Jean Charlot) in the context of Cubism and the Mexican Revolution, now was introduced to Europe by another Frenchman (André Breton), this time in the context of Surrealism and the Occupation.

For a surrealist, it was as much the content as the form of popular imagery which attracted the eye and contained a surrealist charge. Surrealism had a special relationship with the cruel, the morbid and the grotesque. Breton had always loved and praised the works of De Sade, E. T. A. Hoffmann and Lewis Carroll. In creating a counter-tradition to academic classicism and realism, Breton drew heavily on the Gothic and the grotesque. One of his earliest heroes was Alfred Jarry, himself also an admirer and practitioner of the popular print, and in Posada's cuts he saw perhaps an echo of the absurd and horrible world of King Ubu.

Surrealist attitudes and tastes, of course, have permeated European culture, to the point of becoming commonplace and even anodyne. It is hard now not to look at Posada's prints in the way Breton pioneered and see there, first and foremost, the quality which Thomas Gretton has called 'blithe gruesomeness'.[11] Indeed, the appreciation and enjoyment of just such 'blithe gruesomeness' has become acceptable to an extent that would probably have surprised Breton himself, who was still aware of the shock value both of nonsense and of cruelty and morbidity. For Rivera Posada's skeletons and skulls provided a link with the politically repressed world of the Aztecs, were a symptomatic return of values and motifs repressed for centuries by post-Conquest rulers as 'Indian', but for Breton they represented a link with the death instinct, with the repressed impulses of sadism, with the unconscious. Allied to nonsense and to laughter, they threatened the bourgeois order of constraining reason and hypocritical virtue.

From a European viewpoint, the *calaveras* appear as the last, coruscating version of the mediaeval imagery of the *danse macabre*, the Dance of Death. Dating back to the fifteenth century, first appearing in fresco painting, then popularized in woodcuts, the Dance of Death is found, too, in Holbein's prints of 1538. Before 1562 its Lyons publishers had already produced eleven editions and by the end of the century there seem to have been as many as a hundred authorized and unauthorized editions. The Dance of Death drew together strands from the *memento mori* tradition as well as the *danse macabre*, the depiction of a succession of partners for death ranked in order of social precedence, and crystallized a set of responses to the dreadful toll of plague, famine and war. Although it is rarely said, it is hard not to see in the Mexican cult of Posada also a response to the horrors of the revolutionary wars, rather than the prefiguration of their political outcome.

After Holbein, the Dance of Death begins to lose its intensity, the sense of urgency that death may call anyone at any moment, whatever their rank, whatever their wealth, learning or power, from the Pope himself downwards, and the sense of physical decay and destruction that reduces every corpse, however beautiful or strong it once was, to the same stereotypical skeleton with grossly grinning jaws. The Dance of Death becomes a more conventional vehicle for moral tales or satirical lampoons, as with Rowlandson's eighteenth century English version. The Romantic rediscovery of the sublime brought with it, as its shadow and counterpart, the grotesque and the nightmarish, and in Goya's 'Disasters', the Dance of Death is transposed into a different register. It reappears intermittently in its traditional form, but in general it becomes one of the elements in a more generalized art of horror, as with Ensor or Dix. Part of Posada's impact is due to the way in which he recaptures the threads of the traditional form, taking us back once again to the prints of Holbein and his contemporaries. The familiar mediaeval skeletons reappear, but in modern garb, in modern contexts.

'Blithe gruesomeness', however, takes us back not simply to the Dance of Death, which was far from blithe, but to the whole repertoire of nineteenth century urban popular art — catchpenny prints, peepshows, panoramas, Punch and Judy, melodrama and fairground attractions. The heyday of the broadside in Britain came earlier than in Mexico, from the end of the Napoleonic wars onwards, but the material and style were not very different.[12] The prints published by James Catnach at Seven Dials from 1813 to 1838 prefigure those published by Antonio Vanegas Arroyo between 1880 and 1917 in Mexico City. Catnach was phenomenally successful in the same areas as Vanegas — murder sheets, gallows literature, rehashes of famous events, breathless narrations of topical news, chapbooks and so on. He is said to have sold two and a half million copies of his broadsheet on the murderer Rush and to have taken hackney coaches heavy with bags of coppers to the Bank of England.

Catnach's prints, like those of Vanegas, were made to accompany ballads and street-songs, to be hawked at markets and fairs or wherever crowds might gather. Like Posada's work, they show lurid scenes of crime, in which murderers stab their blood-spattered victims with huge knives or demented mothers smash their baby's skull against the wall. Like Vanegas and Posada, Catnach and his artists would use the same print again for a new story. The stress was on grabbing public attention, on gore and melodrama, rather than on naturalistic detail or historical accuracy. In fact, it seems that seventeenth century blocks were still being re-used during the nineteenth century. At other times, blocks would be cut up and re-combined or empty space filled with any available vignette, just as Vanegas and Posada would do.

The subject matter of broadsides also remained more or less constant through the centuries — murders, catastrophes, humour, spectacular political events, sports, etc — and remain so to this day in the sensational press and even now on television. These, of course, were also Posada's staples.

It is interesting to note how the qualities of these prints have affinities with more respectable work, which runs parallel to them and often draws on them or parodies them in a sophisticated way. Thus there is a strong streak of 'blithe gruesomeness' in the work of Edward Lear or, more obviously, Harry Grahame's 'Ruthless Rhymes', which also depend on a combination of comical grotesque doggerel with eye-catching and melodramatic illustrations. Alfred Hitchcock also descends from this tradition and in his work elements from popular imagery, the spectacle of crime and punishment, the fairground, the chamber of horrors and the melodrama are condensed into the narrative mould of the detective and adventure story. Hitchcock began his career as a commercial artist and always prized strong and sadistic visual effects. Posada prints have much in common with a wide range of nineteenth century popular arts in many different countries. For instance, depictions of burning buildings, train crashes and executions were frequent in German *moritaten*, peepshow pictures and panoramas, though these were painted rather than printed and show much more detail. George Grosz remembered seeing in his childhood a panorama of a fire in the Paris *métro* — 'Dozens of tiny scorched fleas rushed the exit in panic fear, while a crushed pile of those trampled down in the rush lay like so many burned matches in the carriage doorways or on the platform. In order to depict the entire gruesome scene the artist had drawn the people as the tiny insects they really are . . .' .[13] Strangely enough, I have seen the same panorama (or one of another *métro* fire in 1903), but I was struck not so much by the insect-like appearances of the fleeing victims, but by their wildly waving arms, very reminiscent of the panic-stricken Mexicans in Posada's earthquake prints. Similarly his print of a volcanic eruption seems very like the panorama of Mont Pelée erupting that Grosz also saw and described, with 'human figures, clearly recognizable, spiralling through the air'.

Fires and railway disasters provided material simultaneously not only for Posada or for the German panorama painters, but also for the builders of Coney Island, the pioneering New York amusement park. In 1904 William H. Reynolds devised his 'Dreamland' park at Coney Island, which contained an electrical and mechanical display of the eruption of Vesuvius, the Galveston Flood and the San Francisco Earthquake, as well as a burning hotel with hysterical guests ('Fighting the Flames') and even 'The Leapfrog Railway' in which two cars full of passengers crash into one another only to find that though 'they have actually collided' one car has leapfrogged on specially designed rails right over the top of the other and the passengers who 'in breathless excitement momentarily anticipated disaster . . . yet find themselves safe and sound'. Exhilarating accidents, thrills and spills are the hallmarks of the Luna Park.[14]

Coney Island reminds us that catchpenny prints and broadsides were not only street art but also fairground art, alongside the rides, the puppet and freak shows, the trestle theatres and the ghost rides. Posada frequently uses the old fairground motif of the jaws of Hell, which goes right back to the literal 'grotesque' of the mannerist pleasure garden of Bomarzo in Italy. The *calavera* too is an element of the fiesta, a popular festivity with puppets, fireworks, special markets, drinking, dancing and extra-sweet 'fairground' food (sugar skulls instead of candy-floss or toffee-apples). It is here, in the Luna Park or on the Day of the Dead, that 'blithe gruesomeness' leaves the realm of black humour and enters that of the carnivalesque, a ritualized realm of licence and role-reversal, in which thresholds and frontiers (as between living and dead) are crossed and effaced.

As Peter Stallybrass and Allon White have argued, 'respectable' society feels a deep ambivalence towards the fairground and the carnival.[15] It needs to expel and to control the 'other' world of popular festivity and misrule, but at the same time it feels a secret fascination with it, projecting there its own disavowed desires. There is both a threat and an opportunity for vicarious excitement. Posada's prints carry some of the same ambiguity, especially as they become art objects and museum pieces. They both threaten the conventions of the art world, transgress its implicit rules and standards, and at the same time reinforce by both revealing and yet holding at a distance, by reinvigorating without overwhelming. In many ways, the art world acts as a mediator between the world of carnival and fairground and the respectable world of high culture. It acts as a conduit, with one extremity in Bohemia, the other in the Academy. In Mexico, the influence of Posada made possible the mix of populism and modernism which the artists of the renaissance wanted. It gave them street credibility, so to speak, while they pursued their monumental ambitions.

Perhaps the artist most similar to Posada is the pioneer French film-maker, Georges Méliès. Méliès was born in 1861, nine years after Posada, and worked as an illusionist and caricaturist before beginning to make films in 1896. His period of success lasted till 1909, when changes in the commercial structure of the nascent cinema industry undermined his position. Méliès had relied on selling films to fairground cinemas, booths set up alongside the rides, freak-shows and other entertainments. Again and again in his repertory of 'primitive' black-and-white films (often hand-tinted) we find echoes of Posada. He featured dancing skeletons and giant skulls, part of the legacy of the phantasmagoria and the magic show, as well as films of earthquakes, volcanoes (Mont Pelée), train crashes, aeronautics, comets, state events, folk-tales and monsters. Like Posada, Méliès was first forgotten, then re-discovered by a later generation. Much of his work was destroyed (indeed, he himself set fire to a store of his own films, not seeing any value in them) or survived only by accident.[16]

Posada and Méliès occupy a peculiar niche in art history, in a particular period of transition. They came after the woodcut and the stage illusion, but before the mass-circulation press and cinema. They were small-scale urban professionals, whose work went to entertain, not so much the masses as the crowd. They come right at the beginning of the age of mechanical reproduction, using up-to-date, even innovatory print techniques, but still tied to old systems of distribution and exhibition, which were swept away in their lifetime or soon after their heyday. They saw themselves as artisans, but in the face of the image industry, they were claimed as ancestors by professional artists — post-cubist painters, surrealist and experimental film makers.

One artist who acknowledged the influence of both Posada and Méliès was S. M. Eisenstein. Eisenstein first saw Posada's work in 1929 in Berlin, in the home of the playwright Ernst Toller, and then soon after he visited Mexico to make a film and saw many more of Posada's 'inimitable pages'. The first film Eisenstein saw, at the age of eight, was Méliès's film with a dancing skeleton horse, presumably *The Merry Frolics of Satan*. Later he thought of Méliès's hand-tinting when he came to work on the colour sequences of *Ivan the Terrible*, and he paid tribute to Posada in the Day of the Dead section of his Mexican film. After all, as he once said, 'I have been attracted by bones and skeletons since childhood. An attraction amounting to a sort of malady'.[17] Eisenstein was fascinated, too, by shock effects, by incidents of bizarre cruelty, by simplified and eye-catching images. He was a devoted collector of caricatures, popular prints and imagery, and recycled his collection in his films, transposing engravings or etchings into film shots. Like the Mexican muralists he drew on the urban carnivalesque tradition and monumentalized it. Like them too he wanted to be both modernist and populist. It is no wonder that he was so fascinated by Mexico and specifically by Posada.

Eisenstein's great theme in his twenties films (*Strike, Battleship Potemkin, October*) was the revolutionary crowd, a dynamic flux. They are dominated by street battles and slaughters and even the working class of *Strike* is pre-Taylor and pre-Ford, semi-artisanal, more like a revolutionary 'city mob' than a disciplined mass. Eisenstein is like the Posada portrayed by Leopoldo Mendez, the artist at work while he looks out through the window at the anti-re-electionist riots in the street outside.[18] E. J. Hobsbawn, in his classic PRIMITIVE REBELS describes how the urban riot became a thing of the past, with industrialization (perhaps he should have said Taylorism and Fordism), with the end of famine and food shortages in the industrialized countries, with changes in the cities themselves, separating the rich from the poor in specialized areas, separating residential, commercial, finance and government centres, developing suburbs, re-developing slums, cutting thoroughfares through popular quarters.[19] Posada belongs to the old city of riots and street crowds, pre-revolutionary but culminating (as in Russia) in the Revolution which eventually transformed it.

The political heroes in Posada's prints are still bandits — rural rather than urban figures, perhaps appealing to the pilgrims and market-goers who travelled into Mexico City from the villages, to the Shrine of the Virgin of Guadalupe or to the market, the Zocalo or the bullring. The world portrayed is that of the urban poor, *lumpen* street people and criminals or victimized artisans. Posada's years in Mexico City were during the time when the main political organizations of the workers were anarchist, and, indeed, the anarchists, followers of Ferres, were particularly strong among the *tipógrafos*, who formed a national Confederation de Artes Graficas in 1912. Ferres was cautious, stressing the need for education and 'consciousness-raising', countenancing militancy only after careful preparation.[20] It is in this kind of context that Posada should probably be placed politically.

It was only after Posada's death, as the revolution gathered momentum, that the Mexican working class began to take clearly militant actions, finally committing itself to armed struggle. Despite Rivera's rhetoric it is highly unlikely that Posada would have identified with Zapata. The urban workers fought with Obregon (as did Orozco, Siqueiros and Dr Atl, in various capacities). But in reality Posada was a pre-revolutionary artist, whose relationship with current and impending events was oblique and enigmatic. Perhaps the most we can say is that he demonstrated a vitality and exuberance which was clearly at odds with the *belle époque* formality and order of the Porfirio Díaz regime. His work gives evidence of a force and energy among the *menu peuple* of Mexico City which already threatens to overspill its allotted bounds. But rather than a force of contradiction in the marxist sense, this was more like a force of excess. In Bataille's terms Posada and his public were fascinated by *l'informe*, the monstrous and marginal which threatened the imposed identity and limits of society.

In the last analysis, Posada's art was not political in the sense that later artists chose to give the term — propagandist, ideologically saturated, or even concerned principally with political themes and myths. It was a narrative art and, for that very reason, touched in all kinds of ways on political issues. Posada's prints did not exist independently. They were accompanied by verbal material of various sorts, mainly news stories or *corridos*, improvised narrative ballads celebrating some folk hero (or villain) or commemorating some exceptional event.[21] Like much popular art, broadside prints were only one element in a complex, hybrid discourse. There was no separation of spheres. Insofar as one code dominated the others, it was the abstract code of narrative, which was realized in different, simultaneous modes. The same story was told, in one striking 'headline' image and then again in a more diffuse and elongated song. For Posada, many of the words (and melodies) were written by Vanegas, and the two should therefore be seen not simply as employer and employee but also as artistic collaborators in a hybrid popular form, the broadside or street gazette.[22]

In fact, it is clear that though Vanegas's style did not change greatly when Posada's predecessor, Manilla retired, Posada's style did change when he began to work for Vanegas. This was not due just to the fact that Vanegas was the entrepreneur, the 'producer', or that he was the more forceful artistic personality. The key element in Vanegas's role is that he stood at the crossroads between the creators (including himself) and the street-sellers (who included his wife and family). In a popular form, this is the crucial position, the point of mediation between the street people, pilgrims and revellers who bought and used the prints and the versifiers and engravers who made them. Of course, the same kind of mediation also occurs in the mass arts, in the industrial spectacle, but there the mediations are much more extended and abstracted. Popular art of the kind produced by Vanegas and Posada involved close contact between producer and user, who were part of the same social milieu.

Thus Posada was working in an interzone between the popular but impersonal forms of the mass media or the muralists (whose work was one-off and whose commissions came from the top down, from government minister, ambassador or powerful capitalist) and the more personal but less popular forms of fine art and specialized production for collectors or connoisseurs. It is clear that the art world constantly draws on the popular arts for material or new forms, particularly at moments of crisis and hence it is no surprise that Posada, who played an important role at the beginning of Modernism is re-discovered again as Modernism is challenged and begins to fragment. Indeed, the evaluation of graffiti art in the seventies is reminiscent in many ways of the re-evaluation of the broadside print. Graffiti art involved a street culture, was seen as an expression of the urban poor and underprivileged, was both public and personalized. Like the print, it was highly stylized, designed to be eye-catching and was repeated, although manually rather than mechanically.

Finally, it is important that, despite the similarities we can see between Posada's work and that of European or North American popular artists, he was nonetheless Mexican. Earthquakes and volcanoes, shoot-outs with the police, the Day of the Dead, are all part of Mexican experience, then and now, and the vigour and exuberance of Posada's work springs from this particular reality. As we look at Posada, or graffiti artists, or the Kalighat painters and Battala print-makers of Calcutta,[23] painters from Shaba or Huxian,[24] haj murals or barber-shop signs, we should take care not to deracinate the work, remove it mentally from its context. Instead, we should use the work to question the institutions and parameters of the Western world, to question its hierarchies, its values, its motives and its cults. Popular Third World art is not necessarily any 'purer', but it is different, it reflects different institutions and values, and its difference, as so often is the case, is inseparable from an imbalance of wealth and power. In this sense, Posada was indeed, as Rivera claimed, the artist of the poor and the dispossessed.

1 POSADA, Antonio Rodriguez, *Mexico 1978*
2 POSADA'S MEXICO, ed. Ron Tyler, *Washington 1979*
3 'Mexican Print-Makers I: Manilla' 'Mexican Print-Makers II: Posada' in ART FROM THE MAYANS TO DISNEY, Jean Charlot, *New York 1939* 'Mexican Prints' 'José Guadalupe Posada: Printmaker to the Mexican People' 'Posada's Dance of Death' in AN ARTIST ON ART, Vol II, MEXICAN ART, Jean Charlot, *Honolulu 1972*
4 EL DIA DE LOS MUERTOS, Maria Teresa Pomar, *Fort Worth 1987*
5 VIVE TU RECUERDO, Robert V Childs and Patricia B Altman, *Los Angeles 1982*
6 AN AUTOBIOGRAPHY, JOSÉ CLEMENTE OROZCO, *Austin 1962*
7 IMAGE OF THE PEOPLE, T J Clark, *London 1973*

8 FRENCH POPULAR IMAGERY, Arts Council of Great Britain (Hayward), *London 1974*
9 THE LUBOK, ed. Alla Sytova, *Leningrad 1984*
10 DIEGO RIVERA, THE CUBIST YEARS, Ramón Favela, *Phoenix 1984*
11 MURDERS AND MORALITIES, Thomas Gretton, *London 1980*
12 THE BROADSIDE BALLAD, Leslie Shepard, *London 1980*
13 SCHILDER BILDER, MORITATEN, ed. Erika Karasek and others, *Berlin (East) 1987* A SMALL YES AND A BIG NO, George Grosz, *London 1982* THE GROTESQUE IN ART AND LITERATURE, Wolfgang Kayser, *Indiana 1963*
14 DELIRIOUS NEW YORK, Rem Koolhaas, *London 1978*
15 THE POLITICS AND POETICS OF TRANSGRESSION, Peter Stallybrass and Allon White, *London 1986*

16 MARVELLOUS MÉLIÈS, Paul Hammond, *London 1974*
17 IMMORAL MEMORIES, S M Eisenstein, *London 1983*
18 LEOPOLDO MENDEZ, Manuel Maples Arce, *Mexico 1970*
19 PRIMITIVE REBELS, E J Hobsbawm, *Manchester 1959*
20 ANARCHISM AND THE MEXICAN WORKING CLASS, John M Hart, *Austin 1978*
21 CORRIDOS & CALAVERAS, Edward I. Tinker, *Austin 1961*
22 'Centenario de la casa editorial de Antonio Vanegas Arroyo' TODOS LOS DIAS, numero 9, May 1980, *Mexico* by Blas Vanegas Arroyo
23 WOODCUT PRINTS OF NINETEENTH CENTURY CALCUTTA, ed. Ashit Paul, *Calcutta 1983*
24 THROUGH OUR OWN EYES, Guy Brett, *London 1986*

LA CALAVERA
☙ DEL EDITOR POPULAR ☙
ANTONIO VANEGAS ARROYO

Esta si es la calavera
del Editor popular,
más fachosa y solamera
como otra nunca han de hallar.

El fué quien nos publicaba
mil primores de poesía,
que nuestra vida endulzaba
y llenaba de alegría

Tenía preciosas historias
que al más triste hacían gozar,
y dejaba en las memorias
un recuerdo singular.

Los alegres sin medida,
leyendo sus oraciones
sentían tan corta la vida
que prendían sus corazones....

Las muchachas que alocadas
por el novio ni dormir
pueden las....enamoradas
y no lo saben decir.

Que le quieren, que le adoran:
no se saben expresar....
y las desdichadas lloran....
el Editor Popular.

Da colecciones preciosas
para poder escoger
de mil cartas amorosas,
la que guste á la mujer.

Y los tratos arreglados
los novios pronto tenían
y prometen que abogados
de Don Antonio serían....

Los niños agradecidos
sus cuentos leyeron ya,
que son tan entretenidos
que los lee hasta su papá....

Y millares de folletos
y bibliotecas enteras,
que llevó á los esqueletos
y á todas las calaveras.

Lo que es de hoy en adelante
el cementerio será
la invitación más galante
que cualquier mortal hará.

Allá encontraréis gustosos
mil lecturas agradables,
mil cuentos maravillosos
y versitos admirables.

Historias estravagantes,
oraciones fervorosas;
sucesos espeluznantes
y comedias muy hermosas.

Allá Don Toncho Vanegas,
como en el mundo hizo igual;
sigue llenando talegas
y aumentando su caudal

Aquí dejó á su hijo Blas,
que entre los vivos rezumba,
pero que remite más
para el país de Ultratumba.

Allá compra hasta el demonio
para escribirle á su diabla,
las cartas que Don Antonio,
de puros amores habla,

Y también vende á la muerte
"reglas pa echar la baraja"
que ella aplica diligente
y á los médicos desgaja....

Y todo aquello es ganar,
allí cualquiera trabaja,
y el Editor Popular,
ni muerto jamás se raja.

Y sigue siempre vendiendo
sus ediciones modernas
y todos siguen leyendo
esas lecturas eternas....
Si tú gustas, valedor,
la dirección te daré,
cuando vayas al panteón
al despacho te enviaré.

Y compras tus calaveras
y cuadernos de canciones,
y jotas y peteneras
que alegran los corazones.
Todo se vuelve gozar
ni quien recuerde la vida.....
y el quien no sepa cantar
no más un cuaderno pida.

Y aprenderá mil cautares
y olvidará con razón
la soledad, los pesares
y tristezas del panteón.
Si este año no quieres ir,
Te esperaré el año entrante
Que cuando vuelva á venir....
¡Tú que estés pata tirante!

CALAVERA
OF THE PEOPLE'S PRINTER
ANTONIO VANEGAS ARROYO

This saucy and elegant
Skeleton here
Is the People's Printer,
To all of us dear.

He published a thousand
Rhymes in verse
That provided relief
From life's unending curse.

He had for sale
The most wondrous stories
That brought joy to the sad
And left lasting memories.

The carefree when
His sermons they read
Were reminded with a jolt
That soon they would be dead.

For the lovelorn lasses
Who try to sleep in vain
And who cannot bring themselves
To tell their swain

That they love and adore him,
Remaining tongue-tied,
The People's Printer
Did conveniently provide

Magnificent albums
Of love-letters by the score
So each could choose
Which pleased her more;

And the young lads got
The go-ahead
And promise to pray
For Don Antonio now he's dead.

The children his stories
Avidly read,
And even their parents
Kept them at their bedhead.

Thousands of volumes
With him he took
So that the skeletons
Would not be short of a book.

From now on the graveyard
Will offer more
In the way of entertainment
Than ever before.

You'll find waiting for you
Pages of pleasure,
Scores of wonderful stories
And poems to treasure,

Exotic adventures,
Pious orations,
Ingenious comedies
And the latest sensations.

As in this life,
In the world of the dead
Don Toncho Vanegas
Prospers and is well-fed.

He left his son Blas
The living to entertain,
But the other world
Provides most of his gain.

Even the devil
To his she-devil proposes
With the amorous letters
Don Antonio composes.

And Death buys his instructions
For 'casting the die',
And puts them in practice,
Giving the doctors the lie.

It brings in the money
And provides jobs for all,
And the People's Printer
Even after death has a ball.

His modern editions
Are still selling well,
And his pamphlets find readers
Even in Hell.

If you desire, my good friend,
I'll give you his address
So when you get to the graveyard
You can go straight to his press,

And stock up with calaveras
And songbooks galore,
And ballads and tangos
To hearten you evermore.

Eternal bliss will be yours
And you'll forget this life so sweet . . .
And if you don't know how to sing,
Just ask for a songsheet.

You'll learn songs by the dozen
And the loneliness and gloom
You soon will forget
Of life in the tomb.

If you don't want to go right now
I'll wait for a year and day,
And when that date comes round
You'd better be on your way!

CHRONOLOGY

1810 A clergyman, Miguel Hidalgo y Costilla, starts the first important popular uprising against Spanish colonial rule in New Spain or Mexico. The day (16th Septémber) he issues his 'Cry of Dolores' — a call for wide-ranging reforms — is today celebrated as Mexican Independence Day.

1821 Mexico achieves independence; a conservative officer assumes power as Emperor Agustin I.

1824 Following a successful republican rebellion (1823), the Emperor is deposed and Mexico acquires its first constitution, providing the legal base for a federal republic. The country continues to be restless and runs through 56 different governments between 1821 and 1861. Banditry flourishes in this political climate, as a means of both social and economic mobility.

1845 US troops occupy Texas (then part of Mexico) leading to war between the two countries in the following year.

1847 EL CALAVERA, one of Mexico's first satirical newspapers, is founded in Mexico City. Within months, the journal is closed down by the authorities and its editors jailed.

1848 As a result of the US-Mexican war, Mexico loses more than half its national territory to the USA. The trauma of military defeat and territorial loss radicalises Mexican politics and gives rise to a new generation of liberals led by Melchor Ocampo and Benito Juárez.

1852 José Guadalupe Posada is born in Aguascalientes, a spa 620 km north west of Mexico City.

1856 Reform laws deprive the Church of its properties (lands and buildings).

1857 A successful rebellion (1854) brings the liberals to power and they draft a new constitution providing for a representative democracy and equality before the law.

The constitution meets with some fierce resistance and the country plunges into civil war.

1861 The liberals, led by Juárez, retake Mexico City. Forces opposing them enlist the help of the French Emperor Napoleon II, whose army invades the country.

The satirical magazine LA ORQUESTA is founded in Mexico City and, within a few years, acquires an international reputation. Its principal artist is Constantino Escalante.

1862 A 17th century convent building — known for its insanitary conditions — in Mexico City is turned into Belén prison.

1863 As French troops advance, Juárez flees the capital. Napoleon III installs Maximilian of Habsburg on the re-established Mexican throne.

1866 Following the end of the North American Civil War (1865) the US government pressurises Napoleon III, in the name of the Monroe doctrine, into withdrawing his troops from Mexico.

1867 Juárez' liberals — the young, famed, and so far loyal military leader Porfirio Díaz among them — defeat Maximilian's troops and shoot the Emperor. Juárez resumes the presidency.

1868 Posada is apprenticed to the printer José Trinidad Pedroza in Aguascalientes.

1871 Juárez is re-elected into office. Díaz heads a revolt which is defeated in the following year.

Dr Atl is born.

Posada contributes cartoons to the newly founded satirical magazine EL JICOTE in Aguascalientes. The local authorities close the magazine within the year.

1872 Juárez dies of heart failure; his vice-president, Sebastián Lerdo di Tejada, is elected into office.

Posada and Pedroza leave Aguascalientes for León, an industrial town closer to Mexico City, where Pedroza opens a new print shop.

1875 Posada marries the 15-year old María de Jesús Vela.

1876 Lerdo is re-elected to the presidency, but Díaz subsequently leads a successful revolt in the name of effective suffrage and no re-election.

Pedroza returns to Aguascalientes and leaves his León print shop to Posada.

1877 Díaz assumes the presidency. He reorganises the army, weakening the power of local commanders. At the same time he strengthens the Rurales, the rural police force, absorbing ex-guerillas and bandits; the force, although never exceeding 2,500 members, is to become a symbol of ubiquitous law enforcement — initially to break down regional resistance to central government, later to counter proletarian unrest.

Press censorship is increasing sharply, and the satirical magazine LA ORQUESTA is closed by the authorities.

1878 The Constitution is amended to allow for re-election of the President and State Governors after an interval of 4 years.

Marcario Romero, former leader of a Catholic grassroots rebellion against the liberal secular state and later celebrated in a popular 'corrido', is shot in a cemetery by rivals.

1880 General Manuel González, a personal friend of Díaz, emerges as president in a rigged election. He instigates many large-scale industrial projects, financed by US and European money. Press censorship is reduced.

Antonio Vanegas Arroyo, Posada's future employer and collaborator, opens his print shop in Mexico City. The artist Manuel Manilla starts working with him two years later.

1883 González's popularity takes a plunge as measures designed to tackle the economic crisis trigger widespread protests. The introduction of the nickel coin, subject to fast devaluation, leads to the nickel riots in Mexico City; the coin is withdrawn by the end of the year but it is to reappear in 1905 under similar circumstances.

The Mexico City-León railway is opened.

The painter José Clemente Orozco is born in Zapotlán Jalisco.

1884 Rigged elections return Díaz to office. He strengthens his dictatorial powers establishing a patronage system that involves chosen state governors and local strongmen. Leaders of the opposition press are assassinated or incarcerated in Belén or San Juan de Ulúa prisons (the latter the most dreaded prison of Mexico, situated on an island off Veracruz, its cells below water level and popularly known as 'barrels' for their size and humidity) where many — if not executed — die of disease. As Díaz's 'law and order' policies pay off, Mexico begins to attract foreign investment on a vast scale. The national railway network grows from 700 km in 1877 to more than 19,000 km in 1910. Posada becomes teacher of lithography in León, in a new programme at the local School of Secondary Education.

1886 The painter Diego Rivera is born in Guanajuato.

Saturnino Herrán, the founder of Nationalistic painting, is born.

1887 The Constitution is changed to allow for two consecutive presidential terms.

1888 Díaz has himself re-elected. Rigged elections regularly give him more than 95% of the votes cast until, and including, the 1910 elections.

The bandit-hero Heraclio Bernal, 'Thunderbolt of Sinaloa', — a former supporter of Juárez who turned to raiding foreign-owned mines after 1876 — is betrayed by a member of his band and killed.

Floods in León leave 20,000 homeless and more than 200 dead.

Posada moves to Mexico City. His work becomes more political over the next few years. Commercial pressures cause him to start working in media other than lithography.

1890 All institutional restrictions on re-election are abolished.

The bicycle is becoming the rage in Mexico City.

1891 Vanegas Arroyo invents the 'Don Chepito Marihuano' character. Posada begins to work with him at about this time.

Ramón Alva de la Canal, pioneer of Modernism in the early 1920's, was born.

1892 The Unión Liberal, Díaz's unity party, adopts an election programme of 'scientific' government, giving economic development and law and order priority over individual freedom. A new generation of advisors, positivist and Darwinist academics and technocrats later called the *científicos* (the scientists) starts to influence Díaz's policies. They later acquire the nickname *'cien tísicos'* — 'the hundred consumptives'.

Students and workers stage large-scale demonstrations and riots in opposition to Díaz, the sole candidate in the presidential election. Their leaders are arrested and shot. Díaz returns to the presidency and from now on personally appoints all members of the federal upper and lower chambers.

An uprising of Indians in the town of Tomochic, triggered by federal troops halting a religious procession, is suppressed with utmost violence.

The notorious bandit Ignacio Parra and his outlaw band are hunted down and killed.

Bruno Martínez and his gang rob a jewellery shop in Mexico City, killing the owner. The robbers are captured and condemned. Martínez subsequently escapes twice, but is overpowered and executed.

1893 Former president Manuel González dies.

A new paper EL DEMOCRATA is closed within months

for denouncing illegal gambling houses protected by the authorities. Among the staff arrested is Jesús Flores Magón.

1894 New legislation removes limits on the concentration of land-ownership, in Mexico's still largely rural economy. As the self-sufficient estates, or *haciendas,* expand and cash crop plantations grow, the rural poor and urban unemployed are frequently rounded up by Rurales and the army to serve as labourers wherever there is a shortage in labour supply. By 1910, 90% of Mexico's rural population is landless and close to starvation.

In an earthquake, causing panic and chaos in the capital, the Metropolitan Cathedral and Belén jail are damaged alongside countless homes.

1895 José Yves Limantour, economist and most prominent *científico*, becomes Minister of Finance.

Manuel Manilla, Posada's predecessor at Arroyo's studio, dies a victim of a typhus epidemic.

The painter Manuel Rodriguez Lozano is born in Mexico City.

More than 100 die in a train derailment near Temamtla.

1896 The only candidate to stand against Díaz in the 1896 and subsequent elections is Nicolás Zúñiga y Miranda. A local eccentric, he 'scientifically' predicts gloomy events such as earthquakes which, to the public's derision, never occur on the envisaged dates. As a rally in support of his 'candidacy' threatens to become a joke at the government's expense, he is imprisoned.

The painter David Alfaro Siqueiros is born in Chihuahua.

The painter Fernando Leal, founder of Nationalism in mural painting and, with Jean Charlot, the first wood engraver in Mexico, is born.

1897 An unarmed artisan, Arnulfo Arroyo, breaks the police cordon surrounding Díaz on Independence Day, and hits the president on the back. Arrested on the spot, he dies of stab wounds at police headquarters that night. There follows a public outcry, and the Chief of Police and other members of the force are detained. The former commits 'suicide' while in custody. This is the only attempt on Díaz's life throughout his dictatorship.

1898 Mexico City's first electricity plant is opened.

The composer Silvestre Revueltas is born in Santiago Papasquiaro, Durango.

1899 The Yaqui Indians, defending their lands in Sonora and resisting — like other Indian communities — 'pacification' campaigns are finally and brutally beaten by forces under the command of General Ramon Corral. Thousands are sold into virtual slavery and deported to the Yucatán and the Valle de Mexico, leaving those in charge of the operation as millionaires.

Mexico City census: 350,000 inhabitants.

Rufino Tamayo, whose paintings synthesize Mexican and European Modernism, is born in Oaxaca.

The painter Fermín Revueltas, who introduces Orphism and Futurism to Mexico, is born in Santiago Papasquiaro, Durango.

1901 A homosexual ball is raided in the capital and 41 are arrested.

1902 The well-known aviator Joaquín de la Cantolla y Rico flies across Mexico City in a balloon.

Leopoldo Mendez is born.

1904 The Unión Liberal propose amendments to the Constitution, extending Díaz's next term to 6 years and re-introducing the post of vice-president, abolished at the beginning of Díaz's rule. Díaz nominates the feared Corral as his running mate. They are both, of course, 'elected'.

1905 Limantour introduces the gold standard. The nickel coin reappears, and many Mexicans fall still further below the poverty line.

Justo Sierra establishes the new Ministry of Fine Arts and Education.

Diastrous floods occur in Guanajuato, killing more than 100 people.

The new, foreign-made clock installed in Mexico City's Cathedral fails to keep the time.

1906 The opposition group 'Regeneración', formed in 1900 by the Flores Magón brothers to revive Juárez' liberalism, publish a manifesto from US exile, calling for radical reform.

A strike at the US-owned copper mines at Cananea is brutally broken up by troops and Texas Rangers; the strikers had demanded that preferential employment of US citizens over Mexicans should cease.

1907 A strike by textile workers in Rio Blanco over the issue of labour organisation ends in a massacre of demonstrators.

A worldwide financial depression accelerates a trend whereby real wages in the still comparatively small industrial sector of the Mexican economy decrease by one quarter between 1898 and 1910.

The drainage and sewerage system for the swamps surrounding Mexico City is completed.

1908 In an interview with a US reporter, Díaz indicates he would welcome opposition parties running candidates in the 1910 elections, to initiate a process of democratisation in the country. General Reyes, contending for the vice-presidency, and his Democratic Party are prosecuted. Reyes accepts a foreign posting from Díaz in 1909. Francisco Madero, leader of the anti-re-electionist party he forms, emerges as the opposition's candidate for the presidency advocating the transition to democracy by strictly legal means.

The Mexican bullfighter Rodolfo Gaona, native of León and just returned from a successful tour of Spain, is gored and badly injured in a fight at Puebla. The Mexican nation holds its breath as he fights for his life for 3 days.

1910 Halley's Comet appears over Mexico City (May), widely interpreted first as a sign of God's blessing of Díaz's rule; later as an omen of the impending revolutionary war.

The Centennial of Independence celebrations, highpoint of Díaz's career, begin on 1 September and last for one month. The highly decorated centre of the capital, cleansed of any signs of poverty, serves as stage and backdrop for sumptuous receptions, balls, a grand procession depicting the history of Mexico and military parades. Millions of pesos are spent on the festivities, and 20,000 people — including many foreign dignitaries — attend.

1911 Madero returns to Mexico (February) to co-ordinate the revolutionary forces. Peasants in the South state of Morelos (who had organised the previous year under the leadership of Emiliano Zapata against the expanding plantations) join the uprising (March).

Students strike in the Academy of Fine Arts against the professors because of their old-fashioned methods.

1913 Madero appoints Huerta to put down a mutiny headed by Felix Díaz, Porfirio's nephew. Huerta — supported by the US ambassador — sides with Díaz and after ten days of vicious fighting in Mexico City (the *Decena Trágica*) causing high civilian casualties, assumes the presidency to restore the *ancien régime* (February). On Huerta's orders, Madero and his vice-president are assassinated two days later. The liberal experiment gives way to a military solution.

First open-air school is placed in Sta Anita Xoclimulco under the direction of the painter Alfredo Ramos Martinas who has just returned from Paris where he studied with Monet. Lasts for only a few months.

Posada has died in January, just prior to these events.

1917 After the most violent battles of the Mexican Revolution have been fought, with the loss of more than one million lives through battle and disease, a new political élite emerges introducing the Constitution which is still in force today.

1919-
1920 Villa, Zapata and Carranza are all murdered.

1921 Jean Charlot discovers Posada's prints.

Re-opening of the open-air school and setting up of new branches.

1922 The Mexican Union of Technical Workers, Painters and Sculptors begins publishing EL MACHETE, a broadsheet that develops into the newspaper of the Mexican Communist Party. EL MACHETE reproduces Posada prints.

Muralism begins in the National Preparatory School.

1925 Jean Charlot writes an article on Posada in REVISTA DE REVISTAS.

1928 The group ¡30 30! is formed by the painters of the open-air schools against academicism.

1929- Diego Rivera portrays Posada in his mural on the history of the Mexican nation in the National Palace, **1930** Mexico City.

1930 The first monograph on Posada is published by Frances Toor, Paul (Pablo) O'Higgins, and Blas Vanegas Arroyo, for MEXICAN FOLKWAYS.

1935 The Taller de Gráfica Popular is founded under the auspices of the Cardeñas government.

1948 Rivera portrays Posada in his mural in the Hotel del Prado building.

1 The Burning of Judas.

DEMONS

AND VIRGINS

3

4

3 Moral Tale of Rafaela Perez.
4 The Earth Swallowing Up José Sanchez for the
  Murder of His Children and His Parents.
5 Making a Hash of the Press (Comment on
  press censorship).
6 Ballad of the Dragon.

FRITANGA PERIODISTICA

¡HORROROSA NOTICIA!

7 Horrifying news! The Sacrilegious Robbery and murder of the Priest in the Parish Church of the Village of Zahuaya, committed by an impious called Celso Flores.

8 Sitting Devil.

9 Horrifying murder! Committed in the city of Tuxpan on the 10th of this month by Maria Antonia Rodriguez who stabbed her compadre to death for refusing to have an illicit affair with her.
(Compadre: the relationship between the mother and the Godfather of her son.)

10 A Woman in league with Satan.

ROBO SACRILEGO

y asesinato del Señor Cura en la Iglesia Parroquial
del pueblo de Zahuaya,
cometido por un impío llamado Celso Flores.

7

¡HORROROSO ASESINATO

Acaecido en la Ciudad de Túxpan el día 10 del pres-
mes y año, por MARIA ANTONIA RODRIGUEZ,
mató á su compadre por no condescender á las rela-
9 nes de ilícita amistad.

10

35

¡TERRIBILISIMO EJEMPLAR!

¡¡¡¡¡ Una Niña calumniadora a quien se llevó el Demonio....!!!

En la ciudad de San Cristóbal las Casas, (Estado de Chiapas) vivía con su mamá una niña de doce años de edad, llamada Cenobia. La madre llamábase Doña Mariana. La niña mencionada había quedado huérfana de padre, desde la edad de tres años. La madre no se ocupó nunca de educar a Cenobia ni en la moral ni en nada. Con las niñas y niños y hasta con la gente grande andaba siempre en chismes y revolturas; su gusto era poner a reñir a todos diciéndoles que hablaban mal unos de otros. La calumnia era su cuerda principal como dicen.

Y como estaba tan consentida por la madre, esta nunca la castigaba, a pesar de conocer muy bien sus malísimas costumbres. Ni siquiera le daba consejos. Doña Mariana pensaba que aquellas maldades de calumniar y predisponer a las gentes, era resultado de su viveza. Y naturalmente, aquella niña cada día estaba peor; varias veces hasta se habían registrado crímenes por causa de sus chismes y calumnias. Las personas a quienes les

decía mentiras para que se pelearan, pensaban erróneamente como la generalidad en aquel refrán tonto que dice: «Los locos y los muchachos dicen las verdades.» Y esta creencia la sostenía siempre dándole completa acogida. No reflexionaban que en todo lo contrario, pues los locos y los muchachos son los que mienten más.

Pero vamos ya a narrar el espantosísimo caso que tuvo lugar como palpable ejemplo, tanto para las niñas como para las madres. La última calumnia inventada por Cenobia fué la que la llevó a la completa perdición de su alma. Sucedió que en la casa donde Cenobia vivía con su mamá, habitaba a la vez un matrimonio sin hijos, el esposo se llamaba Raymundo y era sastre; la esposa Eduviges.

Raymundo era muy quisto con su mujer y esto lo sabía muy bien Cenobia. Antes de continuar diremos, que esta niña tenía alcances y comprensión de gente grande así es que estaba al tanto de la vida privada de los vecinos. A Eduviges no la quería nada, la

12

MUY INTERESANTE NOTICIA

De los cuatro asesinatos por el desgraciado Antonio Sánchez
en el pueblo de San José Iturbide,
Estado de Guanajuato, quien después del horrible crimen, se comió los restos de su propio hijo.

11 A terrible lesson: a girl slanderer is carried away by the Devil.
   This broadside describes how Cenobia, the twelve year old daughter of Dona Mariana, loved to slander people that she knew, turning them against one another. One day she told Raymundo, a tailor who lived next door, that a young student was visiting his wife each day while he was at work. He believed her. The following week a student came to his house to ask him to make him a suit but Raymundo didn't bother to speak to him, instead blasting both the student and his wife with six shots from his pistol.
   That night Cenobia had what she thought was a dream: the devil came, and took her away saying, "I'll take you, because you serve me; you are the best slanderer in the world." Suddenly she realised that it was no dream and that she was, indeed, being spirited away to hell.

12 Poor old 1895

13 OVERLEAF: Very interesting news of the four murders by the unfortunate Antonio Sanchez in the village of San José Iturbide in the State of Guanajuato, who, after the horrible crime, ate the remains of his own son.
   This broadside tells the story of Antonio Sanchez who lost the title to his farm, probably through gambling. He came home to get the deed, but his old parents refused to give it to him because they realised the gravity of his sin. Sanchez went mad, grabbed the hatchet in the corner of the room and killed his father, his mother and his wife. He then cut his infant son into four pieces with two blows of the hatchet. He then ate the remains of his son. Neighbours raised the alarm and Sanchez was arrested and sentenced to be shot and then hanged to serve as an example to others who might consider committing the same crime.

14

15

14 Great Fright: Apparition of
   Pachita the Nougat Vendor.
15 Love and Death.
16 *(The seven deadly sins)*
   Ghostly Death Shakes the Town
   of Silao in the Opening Days of
   the Twentieth Century. Wealthy
   Man Commits Suicide Out of
   Envy!
17 Untitled.

16

17

18 Sensational and Gruesome Parricide Committed in El Saltillo on the First of Last Month, A Warning to Us All!

19 Moral Tale: Heartless Daughter Murders Beloved Parents.

20 The metal plate for 18 (enlarged).

SENSACIONAL NOTICIA
LA CONFESION DE UN ESQUELETO
UNA ALMA EN PENA
DENTRO DEL TEMPLO DEL CARMEN

21

21 News Sensation! Skeleton Seeks Confession! Ghost in the Templo del Carmen

22 Hallucinations of a Drunk.

22

Espectros y aparecidos.

Fantasmas en Santo Tomás.

UN LOCO MONOMANIACO

Y Pachita la alfajorera.

Boca abajo las antiguas leyendas del «Callejon del Muerto,» del «Padre Lecuona,» del «Padre Lanchitas,» de la «Calle de Olmedo» y tantas y tantas otras, que narradas por nuestras cariñosas abuelas, cuando éramos niños, nos ponían los pelos de punta y nos hacían buscar en el lecho, bajo las sábanas y dominados por un terror soberbio, un refugio que nos pusiera á salvo de aquellos fantasmas que veíamos flotar en la atmósfera de nuestra impresionada imaginacion!

Lo repetimos, ¡boca abajo esos espantos! ¡Vuestro padre está ahí! Digo mal; vuestra madre, porque ahora es una *espectra* la que ha venido á empequeñecer á las adormidas y casi olvidadas leyendas de antaño.

Una celebridad popular fué la generálmente conocida P*achita*, vendedora de alfajores, celebridad que por cierto no alcanzó por lo exquisito y bien hecho de su mercancía, sino por su original modo de pregonarla, con un *canto* que partía medio á medio lo ménos armónico que en música pueda existir, y por aquella boca, como vulgarmente se dice, que era el más abastecido almacen de insolencias que ponía siempre á disposicion del público, hubiera ó no razon para que se desbordara ese raudal de frases escogidas....entre las peores; pues en *Pachita* era característico un génio díscolo é irasible como pocos.

Yo conocí á *Pachita* hace cuando ménos 20 años y estaba enteramente lo mismo que hace poco más de un año que dejé de verla y llegué á sospechar que se había convertido en fósil; pero no hubo tal, y segun cuenta la crónica hace un año poco más ó ménos entregó el espíritu en un hospital.

Y aquí entra lo grave.

Un año despues, el dia 2 del actual el fantasma de la célebre alfajorera hizo su primera visita de aparecida á este mundo presentándose en su antiguo domicilio, 2ª calle de Santo Tomás la Palma, casa núm. 9, cuarto número 9.

Habitaba en esta fecha el histórico cuartucho, un pobre nevero llamado Paulo Martinez que cayó en gracia al chocarrero espíritu alfajorero para cojerlo de su cuerva coja, comenzando por presentársele en su clásico traje.

No le faltaba nada; ni el sombrero de anchas alas y elevada copa, ni el rebozo terciado y anudado sobre la cadera

No agradaron á Paulo esas visitas y trató de cambiar su domicilio, pero el espectro se opuso y no le dejaba desocupar la pieza y sin duda para castigarlo por su abandono, tuvo el capricho de entretenerse en quitarle el bote de la nieve que vendia Martinez, y derramar en el suelo el contenido, y esto muchas veces en presencia de los compradores que veían volar el susodicho

bote y demás adminículos, impulsados por una mano invisible para todos, excepto para el nevero que muy distintamente veía á su perseguidor fantasma.

Malas, muy malas caminaban las cosas para Martinez que comenzó á enflaquecer á ojos vistas y á ponerse más amarillo que el Vientre del Siglo, ó el Siglo Vientre que lo es desde el idem de la que le dió el ser, pero aún se pusieron peor, pues parece que el espectro aquel se envalentonó y dió principio á peores tratamientos.

Se dice que Pachita había hecho su caja fuerte en el pozo de la casa donde depositaba sus ahorros y queriendo que Paulo fuera su heredero se empeña en llevar á aquel infeliz al citado depósito, y esto á fuerza de tiron limpio.

Lo más espantable de tan espantoso espanto, está en que en presencia de personas extrañas, éstas pueden ver cómo el cuerpo de Martinez que se desmaya á la aparicion del espectro, es arras-

trado por una fuerza invisible.

Y cuenta la historia que al fin lograron los parientes del espantado, sacarlo de aquel antro y conducirlo á una accesoria retirada de la mansion aquella, pero no por eso ha quedado libre de la persecucion, pues á la hora fatal, el fantasma se presenta y car-

gando el desmayado cuerpo de Paulo, lo conduce por los aires al fatídico cuarto, y esto burlando la vigilancia de una multitud de amigos y parientes que acompañan á la víctima de las chocarrerías del chancero espíritu de Pachita la alfajorera.

La estúpida conseja ha sido desgraciadamente creída y aceptada de buena fé, por la no tan escasa ignorancia de multitud de gente que tan sólo de oir la estupenda narracion de tales prodigios, se muestra aterrorizada, afirmándose más en su obcecacion y tomando pié para creer en la infalibilidad de ese suceso, en el hecho de que, segun se afirma, el cuarto ha sido exorcisado por sacerdotes, con objeto de ahuyentar la aparicion.

Lo que es un hecho cierto y positivo, es que el *espantado* Paulo Martinez, que habita hoy una accesoria del Puente del Blanquillo, está muriendo consumido por una alucinacion fatídica quizas incurable, pues léjos de que se le aplique una curacion que pudiera salvarlo, no tiene á su lado sino alicientes que aumentan la calentura de su cerebro.

Lo que más espanta en este espantoso espanto es la credulidad espantosa de nuestro pueblo.

A última hora se nos dice que Martinez ha sido llevado á la Inspeccion respectiva, para que el médico lo observe.

Vea usted la cuarta plana

24   **Los espantos de la Amargura**

25

---

23 Ghosts and Apparitions. The spectre of St Thomas Street. Obsessed Lunatic and Pachita the Candy-Seller.

24 Apparition at La Amargura.

25 Textual illustration from the story *The Manslayer*.

23

SOL EN ESCORPION

—¿Quién causa mas agonías
Y mas fuerte sofocon
Que.el venenoso escorpion?
¿Quién? ¡pues cualquier Matatías!

26 Sun in Scorpio
    What causes more pain and anxiety
    than a venomous scorpion?
    A Moneylender!

VERDADERO
Y ASOMBROSO MILAGRO,

Que Ntra. Sra. de Guadalupe, hizo en favor de un devoto suyo en uno de los últimos dias del mes próximo pasado.

Era Silvestre García carnicero de oficio y ardientísimo devoto de Nuestra Señora de Guadalupe, á la que siempre se encomendaba con gran fé.

Habitaba en una ranchería llamada Maocavaca, del Estado de México, ocupando una humilde habitación en compañía de su familia.

Dormían una noche tranquilamente, recogidos desde las primeras horas, cuando á eso de las ocho, despertó á Silvestre la voz de su hijo Marcelino que con acento que cada vez se hacia más apagada, exclamó:

—¡Papá! me están ahorcando!......... ¡Ah! me ahorcan! ¡Ah!

Al despertar Silvestre, lo primero que se figuró fué que los ladrones se hubieran introducido á su vivienda y por eso se armó de su afilado cuchillo y encen-

diendo una luz buscó en la pieza á los facinerosos: pero sólo vió á toda su familia entregada á profundo sueño y creyendo entonces que los gritos hubieran venido de afuera, iba á salir de la casa, pero al pasar para la puerta, vió el rostro de su hijo Marcelino renegrido y advirtió que boqueaba y que sus ojos se volteaban con angustia indecible. Se inclinó entonces sobre él y descubrió que tenía enredado al cuello un objeto que le daba tres vueltas. Era una especie de gruesa reata, de un color amarillo plomizo con manchas negras.

Con el espanto que es fácil concebir, conoció en aquel objeto una víbora de cascabel de la más peligrosa clase.

Su primer pensamiento fué invocar á la milagrosa Virgen de que era devoto, y luego despertó á su mujer y á sus de-

28 Theatre of Illusion: Advertisement for a fairground
attraction. (Originally printed in 1903 programme
for the Arbeu Theatre, advertising a play with
special effects: *Love Conquers All, or The Devil's
Hindleg*).

29

30

31

29 Amazing True Miracle
Performed by our Lady
of Guadalupe for a
Devout Worshipper at
the end of Last Month.
30 The New Messiah.
31 Portrait of His
Excellency Dr
Próspero M Alarcón
on His Consecration as
Archbishop.
32 Appearance of the
Virgin of Guadalupe at
Los Remedios.

32

33

33 Album of
   Love Letters,
   Book 7.
34 Songbook
35 The Steam
   Engine, from
   Modern
   Songbook.
36 Album of
   Love Letters,
   Book 8.
37 Untitled.

34

35

54

LOVE

37

38

39

EL CASAMIENTO DE LOLITA

40 PAPA Y MAMA DECIDEN DE SU PORVENIR

41

38 Duck Duet.
39 Ballad of the Snake Woman. *'So that's the way you'll trap me . . .'*
40 Lolita Gets Married. Mother and Father Decide Her Fate.
41 A Folly. Father Cobos and Doña Caralampia Dance a Merry Can-Can.

TIERNAS SUPLICAS
con que invocan las jóvenes de Cuarenta Años
AL MILAGROSO
S. ANTONIO DE PADUA
PIDIENDOLE SU CONSUELO

42 TENDER ENTREATIES

WITH WHICH YOUNG GIRLS
FORTY YEARS OF AGE INVOKE THE
MIRACLE-WORKING ST. ANTHONY
OF PADUA PRAYING TO HIM FOR
COMFORT.

Oh miraculous St. Anthony,
Look on these tears which I shed
I pray you give me a husband
Because I am overripe.

St. Anthony beatific,
Oh Saint of my fervent prayer,
Give me, for pity, a husband
And release me from this care;
Aged, one-armed, paralytic,
Either with or without his hair,
Just as long as he will have me —
A soldier of any type;
All I want is to get married
Because I am overripe!

I do not ask for a general,
A marquis, count, or a duke;
All that I want is a man
Who'll give me a second look;
I don't care if he's a robber
Or some other kind of crook,
Do you not see how I suffer
In the cruel, maternal gripe?
A husband, oh dear St. Anthony,
Because I am overripe!

Most compassionate of saints,
I ask you with hope devout
That you will give me a mate,
No matter the shame or doubt;
If there is no other way
An old man, perhaps, with gout,
Since the others run so fast;
Oh, Saint, please get me a fellow!
Have pity on this poor woman,
Because I am more than
mellow!

Most blessed St. Anthony on high,
In the celestial city,
In your infinite might
Take pity, oh take pity.
How about an ageing widower
To leave me sitting pretty?
Thwart not my urgent need,
Help me plight my troth
Even if it's to the Devil,
Before I start to go off.

San Antonio milagroso
Yo te suplico llorando
|| Que me des un buen esposo
Porque ya me estoy pasando

San Antonio bendecido,
Santo de mi devoción,
Por tu santa intercesión
Dame, por Dios, un marido
Sea viejo, manco ó tullido,
Que me quiera en todo caso,
Y sí no un soldado raso,
O un recluta de cuartel,
¡Para casarme con él:
¡Que me paso! ¡que me paso!

No te pido un general,
Duque, conde ni marqués:
Que lo que yo quiero es,
Un hombre que sea formal.
Sea el ladrón más criminal,
El caso es tener marido.
Ya ves cuanto he padecido
En el materno regazo.
¡Oh San Antonio querido!
¿No ves, que me paso?

Santo misericordioso,
Te lo pido y en tí espero,
que me des un compañero,
¡Un esposo, un buen esposo!
Aunque sea viejo gotoso,
Nada me importa el frentazo
Porque nadie me hace caso,
Me huyen como á lucifer;
Piedad para esta mujer,
¡Mira, santo, que me paso!

Por tu santa caridad,
¡Oh, San Antonio bendito!
Ten de mí piedad, piedad,
Por tu poder infinito.
Dame siquiera un viudito
Que me dé un buen difuntazo;
En este difícil caso,
Arregla mi matrimonio,
Cásame con el demonio
Porque si no, yo me paso!

43 Ah, That Lovely Simona, Hard to Handle and what a Mug! 44 Loose Ends. 45 The Farmer and the Sparrowhawk. 46 Rising to the Occasion.
47 The Verbena de la Paloma (a popular fiesta).

49

50

51

48

52

48 Love Story Under Umbrella.
49 Woman Embracing a Man.
50 Painful Parting from the Whores in the Callejón de López.
51 A Binge.
52 Back from the Walk.
53 Dancing Farmers.
54 Flirting.

53

54

55

55 A Bluebeard.

56 Amorous Conversation Between a Sly Cobbler and a Brazen Pussy Cat.

57 The Revolutionary's Farewell.

58 Detail from *Calaveras of Licentious and Saucy Serving Wenches.*

59 Woman and Old Man After the Dance.

60 Tales from Beyond the Grave: *Love*, a Spiritualist Romance by Luis Kortey: Dreams and Nightmares Scientifically Explained.

61 Visit to the Theatre.

56

57

58

59

60

61

41 MARICONES PARA YUCATAN,

Las impresiones de viaje—Resaladas
cual no hay más—De todos los maricazos
Que mandan á Yucatán.

Sin considerar tantito
A nuestro sexo tan casto,
Ni el estado interesante
Que casi todas guardamos,

Hechas horrible jigote
A todas nos encajaron
En un carro de tercera
Del *transote* Mexicano.

Revueltas cual chilaquiles
Fuimos con jergas soldados
Que injuriaban leperotes
Nuestro pudor con descaro.

Al pobrecito Soflo
Le dieron muchos desmayos
Con los continuos meneos
De este tren tan remalvado.

63

LOS 41 MARICONES

Encontrados en un baile de la Calle de
la Paz el 20 de Noviembre de 1991

Aquí están los Maricones

MUY CHULOS Y COQUETONES.

Hace aun muy pocos días
Que en la calle de la Paz,
Los gendarmes atisbaron
Un gran baile singular.

Cuarenta y un lagartijos
Disfrazados la mitad
De simpáticas muchachas
Bailaban como el que más.

La otra mitad con su traje,
Es decir de masculinos,
Gozaban al extrechar
A los *famosos jotitos*.

Vestidos de raso y seda
Al último figurín,
Con pelucas bien peinadas
Y moviéndose con chic.

62

62 The 41 Homosexuals Caught in the Act at a Ball on la Paz Street on 20 November 1891. Here are the Queens parading their Charms.
63 Deportation of the Queers to Yucatan. Naughty Impressions of their Journey.

64 For the Ladies.
65 Theatres.
66 Hard-times Dance.

67 The Coal
Shortage.
(plate)

68

69

70

GRAN COMETA Y QUEMAZON,

QUE MUY PRONTO SE VA A VER:

EL MUNDO SE VA A VOLVER
TODITITO CHICHARRON.

¡El mundo se va á acabar! Nos vamos á tostar irremisiblemente! ¡Qué á tostar! Ya quisiéramos! ¡A volvernos ceniza!

Un gran astrónomo de Europa lo ha predicho últimamente; ya no para Noviembre del año de 1899, sino para el mes de Octubre próximo. Esta catástrofe horrorosísima la va á anunciar el cometa gigantesco que aparecerá en estos días; este astro malévolo será el que chocará con la tierra, haciendo mil averías, por

71

68 Satire on the Comet of 1889.

69 Watching the Comet.

70 The End of the World Has Come! Rain of Stars and Comets.

71 GIANT COMET AND UNIVERSAL CONFLAGRATION COMING SHORTLY! THE WHOLE WORLD ABOUT TO BE BURNT TO A CINDER!

The end of the world is nigh! We are doomed to roast! Nay, be turned to ashes!
According to the forecast of a famous European astronomer, the date is no longer set for November 1899 but for this coming October. The frightful catastrophe will be heralded by the imminent appearance of a giant comet, which same ill-omened star will collide with the earth, wreaking universal havoc . . .

72 Moral Tale of Bruno Ramirez

72

73 THE FREAK
HAILSTORM OF
9 APRIL 1904.
The Fury of the
Elements Unleashed!
Property Wrecked!
Dead and Injured!

LA TERRIBLE GRANIZADA

DEL 9 DE ABRIL DE 1904.

¡Furibunda tempestad, Desplomes, Muertos y Heridos!

El 9 de Abril de este año,
En la Capital de México,
Como á las tres de la tarde
Dió principio el gran siniestro.
 Fué oscureciendo por grados
Hasta haber necesidad
De encender el alumbrado
En tiendas de la ciudad,
 Poco después comenzaron
Gruesas gotas á llover.
Y dentro pocos momentos,
Granizo empezó á caer.
 Desde hace nueve años no hubo
Granizada como esta
Provino del lado Sur.
Y fué de lo más horrenda
 En las calles se miraba
Lo mismo que en azoteas,
Cubierto por todas partes
De aquellas heladas piedras.
 Pedazos muchos se hicieron
Tragaluces y vidrieras
Y también aparadores
Del granizo con la fuerza.
 Obstruyéronse los caños
Del desagüe de azoteas,
Y el líquido se filtró
En las casas y las tiendas
 Se perdieron ricas telas,
Muebles y también tapices;
Se inundaron las bodegas
Y hubo conflictos á miles.

Muchos jardines públicos
Y macetas de las casas
Se arruinaron por completo
Con aquella granizada.
 Entre muchos accidentes,
Que el granizo ocasionó,
El más importante fué,
El que está á continuación.
 Fué el Mercado conocido,
De «Martínez de la Torre,»
El techo se vino abajo
Causando serios temores.
 Cuando el siniestro se hallaba
En su completo apogeo,
Dos eléctricas descargas
Se oyeron con gran estrépito.
 Un rayo cayó veloz
Por una calle de Zarco,
Y el otro por Occidente
En la calle de Doblado.
 Por fortuna en esto no hubo
Desgracias que lamentar,
Sólo sustos, muchos sustos,
Como es fácil de pensar.
 Donde si hubo fué á la caída
Del Mercado de "La Torre"
Dos muertos allí quedaron
Con el terrible desplome.
 Fué uno Ascensión Rodríguez
Velador de aquella Plaza,
Y el niñito Luis Jiménez
Que á Ascensión acompañaba.

74

75

74 Sublime Creator of Heaven and Earth, Deliver Us
    from Another Earthquake.
75 The Hecatomb of Chalchicomula.
76 Ballad of the Temamatla Derailment.

76

FIN DE LA FABRICA DE CERILLOS
"LA ORIENTAL."
►EL INCENDIO DEL MARTES◄

LA CATASTROFE
EN EL FERROCARRIL DEL SUR

Ampliando la noticia que publicamos ayer con relacion á aquel sensible acontecimiento, diremos que el tren de pasajeros que salió de Puebla rumbo á Oa-

micilio ó continuaron en marcha, por lo que me es imposible listarlos. Iban para Tehuantepec Inocencio Peña, mayor de 10° y hermana Casimira, quienes se c

77

78

SINIESTRO EN UN TALLER.
Las víctimas del trabajo

79

77 End of the Match Factory *La Oriental* in Tuesd
    Fire.
78 Train Crash on the Southern Railway.
79 Accident in a Sweatshop. The Victims of Labou
80 Universal Final Judgment! End of the World to
    Place on 14 November 1899 at 45 Minutes Pas
    Midnight!

EL GRAN JUICIO UNIVERSAL!

¡¡Fin de todo el Mundo para el 14 de Noviembre de 1899 á las 12 y 45 minutos de la noche!!

Para el día 14 de Noviembre del presente año de 1899. está anunciado con todas las formalidades debidas y muy circunstanciadamente el terrible "Fin del Mundo." Muchos, muchísimos lo han creido; pero por fortuna no va á suceder nada del horripilante cataclismo; todo va á resultar farsa en cuanto al terremoto y lluvia de piedrotas incandescentes, las cuales ya parece que descalabran calaveras y hasta sienten algunos el dolorcillo consiguiente, como si ya les hubiera roto la *pensadora*, El renombrado austriaco, el eximio astrónomo Rodolfo Falb se ha equivocado lamentablemente, según la más autorizada y respetable opinión del gran astrónomo frances Camilo Flammarión: Rodolfo Falb dijo que el día 14 de Noviembre próximo á las doce y cuarenta y cinco minutos de la noche se hallará en el espacio la Tierra y el cometa nombrado de Biela descubierto hace muy poco tiempo. La desconsoladora profecia, el aterrador cálculo hecho con siniestro laconis-

á la nerviosa y espantada humanidad. "El 14 de Noviembre del presente año de 1899--dice Mr. Flammarion—desde el mediar de la noche al amanecer, se efectuará una sorprendente lluvia de estrellas erráticas ó exhalaciones procedentes de la constelación llamada "Leo." Estas son las famosas «Leonidas» que debieron ser vistas el 14 de Noviembre de 1898 y que no aparecieron á nuestras miradas por la lógica y excelente razón de encontrarse entonces á la muy respetable distancia de 745 millones de kilómetros á la tierra. El lujosísimo conjunto de meteoros describe una órbita elíptica alrededor del sol, invirtiendo en dicho viaje unos 33 años. Tan maravilloso fenómeno pudo ser observado en los años de 1766, 1799, 1833 y 1866, por más que en esta última fecha el número de estrellas erráticas se había reducido grandemente. Razones tengo para asegurar que esa disminución se hará palpable ahora, pues he mostrado que las referidas «Leonidas» pueden observarse to-

como saben todos los astrónomos, el espacio está abastecido de cometas que, por decirlo así, revolotean al rededor del sol cual un enjambre de mariposítas alrededor de una vela encendida ú otra luz. Como es natural, al efectuar la tierra su movimiento de translación, es decir, de un lado á otro, está expuesta á tropezar con cualquiera de los referidos cometas. Suponiendo que así sucediese, el choque de nuestro planeta, la Tierra, la lluvia de exhalaciones, que produjera, no tendría ninguna consecuencia grave. Precisamente la aproximación que vaticina Mr. Falb se verificó en el año do 1832, el día 29 de Octubre; el cometa de Biela fué uno de los que cruzaron la órbita de la Tierra, sin causar otra cosa más que el temor, sin fundamento, por las profecías de los astrónomos

Si hubiera entonces ocurrido el choque, naturalmente en aquel tiempo se habrían ocasionado múltiples desgracias, porque ha de recordarse que marchó nuestro planeta á una

81

82

83

¡FUEGO!

84 Heroísmo del Bombero.

81 Ballad of Electric
   Road Accidents.
82 Hecatomb of
   Chalchicomula. A
   True Story.
83 The Floods of León.
   Modern Songbook.
84 Fire! The Heroic
   Fire Brigade.
85 Fire Sweeps the Sweet
   Factory *Los Pirineos*.
86 Fire at the Chicago
   Exhibition.

85   Incendio de la fábrica de dulces "Los Pirineos."

SE APROXI

LAS PROF

Temblores,

Guerras, Pest

87 The Coming of the End of the World: Prophecies Come True. Earthquakes, Eruptions, Wars, Plagues, Famines and Fires.

A EL FIN DEL MUNDO

CIAS SE CUMPLEN

Erupciones,

, Hambres e Incendios.

DON CHEPITO MARIHUANO

88

89

90

91

88-93 Don Chepito Marihuano, a character invented by Arroyo and Posada, in different madcap situations.

92

93

94 Suicide.

PRIVATE CONFLICTS

95 Sparks.

AND SUICIDES

LAMENTATIONS
OF A DRUNK
OVER THE CLOSING
OF SALOONS
AND PULQUE SHOPS.

The Devil may take us now!
I am done! I'm really sunk!
After twelve o'clock on Sunday
I'm forbidden to get drunk.

All the pulque shops will close,
And the saloons as well;
And so to water we're driven
Like oxen, our thirst to quell.

And me, who with my guitar
Would go on a Sunday morn
To down a couple of measures
As big as bushels of corn.

And after some versifying
Would follow a little fight;
Then to jail with my buddies
For a warm and pleasant night.

Damn! But they fixed us good!
It would be better to kill us
Than to take from us this way
The nectar that used to fill us.

The fine tequila, the brandy,
And all other kinds of liquor;
The Devil take us, Señor,
They sure could have killed us quicker

They want us to freshen up,
As if it were summer. Lord!
When the frijoles we eat
Leave us as stiff as a board.

They took our covers away,
Those that covered us within;
And now we must take to water
And shiver inside our skin.

And water it then must be,
No matter how foul or smelly;
We'll be breeding toads and snakes
And even sharks in our belly.

So now we are fresh enough,
As fresh as the morning dew;
You must learn to bear it, brother;
There is nothing we can do.

Last night at the old liquor palace
As I was leaving the same —
Once the haunt of thieves and robbers
It keeps its early fame —

I was sweating like the Devil
And so thirsty that I neighed;
So what could I do but order . . .
A glass of cold lemonade!

Los Lamentos de un Borrachito
Con motivo del cierre de Pulquerías y Cantinas.

¡Pos hora sí me amolé!
Nos va á llevar la *disgracia*;
Los domingos á las doce
Ya se acabó la parranda.

Se cierran las pulquerías
Y las cantinas también,
Y á retragar purita agua,
Purita agua como *guey.*

Yo que los domingos iba
Con mi *guitarra* á pasear,
Encachándonos medidas
Hartas, hartas como maiz.

Y allí á versarl ., manario,
Y á pelearnos tan bonito,
Y luego á la Tlapisquera
Para dormir calientito

¡Caray, caray, me amolé!
Mejor, mejor nos mataran,
Y no quitarnos así
Así nomás el Tlamapa.

Y luego hasta el refinito
Y toditito licor,
Pos nos va á llevar el diablo,
Nos va á llevar sí patrón

Se emperran en refrescarnos
Como si hiciera calor,
Pos que no ven que el *frijol*
Nos deja tiesos, *siñor?*

Nos quitaron la *cobija*
La cobija de por dentro;
Ya nos tocó ia hora mala
Y agua solo beberemos.

Agua aunque sea del Drenaje,
Agua de puros *maclovios*
Que se nos *güelvan* culebras
Y sapos y *tiburonos.*

Pos hora sí estamos *frescos*,
Frescos deveras, caray!
Y hay que aguantarnos manito
Ni modo de repelar.

Salí anoche de las tandas
Del jacalón del Tepache,
Que solo el nombre le queda
Porque no más hay *germanes.*

Tenía una sed de los diablos,
Y estaba sudando....¡tinta!
Y, que otro *rimedio?* Así
Un vaso de horchata fría.

VERSOS DE LINO MATADAS
QUE NI AL DIABLO TIENE MIEDO,
Y SABE DAR CUCHILLADAS
NOMAS CON EL PURO DEDO.

97 Verses of Lino Matadas
    Who fears not Hell
    And with his little finger
    Any adversary can fell

★ The same plate as 96 with an
additional figure.

Por donde quiéra que hay modo
Entra haciendo santiaguitos,
Se enreda á los borrachitos
Que traigan su momo meodo.
A un barbero medio bobo
Le dió tal arrempujón
Que lo dejó sin calzón
Y con la pierna abollada,
Le dió su buena nalgada
Y una zurra, de pilón.

Este entra por donde enfade,
Arrebata á las fonderas,
Les quiebra hasta las cazuelas
Y no les deja ni madre.
Y dice aunque no le cuadre
Que lo tire y monte en pelo;
Entró en casa de un abuelo
A encacharse su traguito
Y como no dió prontito
Me le sonó las de cuero.

¡Ay chibarras coloradas!
Gritó en la mera placita,
Y como había funcioncita
Les dió muchas puñaladas.
Pues les tiró rebanadas
Como si fueran melón,
Y agarrando al del pistón
Me le dió tal sacudida
Que le hizo echar la comida
Y bailar el rigodón.

A la tienda del Aguaje,
Se metió sin tón ni són,
Y le sonó un pescozón
Al dependiente por maje;
Y le dijo «¡no se raje!»
Oigasté, Don Catrincito,
Encáchese ese pulquito
Pero ya, luego, prontito
Aunque sea un sólo trago,
Porque si no lo calillo.

LAS "LECHUZAS"

98

99

100

CONFLICTO PRIVADO
por no usar estas Pildoritas

101

102

LOS DRAMAS DE LA MISERIA.

Un lanzamiento.

103

104

98 The Shrews
99 The Shrews
100 Getting Home
101 Domestic Tiff All Because of Not Taking Those Pills.
102 A Dispute with the Mother-in-Law.
103 Dramas of Poverty. An Eviction.
104 Popular Customs.

105

106

105 End of the Orgy. **106** Neighbours Quarrel.

Loa dicha por Sancho Panza y Doña Cenobia.

EN HONOR

de la Pureza de María Santisima.

MUSICA.

Todos en unión cantemos
La Pureza de María,
Pues la celebramos hoy
Con gusto y con alegría.

*Sale Sancho Panza con una talega al la-
do izquierdo. en la que trae cosas de comer y una botella, y en el brazo derecho
una olla de migas; el que aparecerá ba-
rrigón y colorado. Poniendo en el suelo
la olla y limpiándose el sudor, dice:*

Pues señor, no hay que dudarlo,
Nadie me ha de convencer,
Que el gusto mayor del mundo
No hay otro como el comer.
Es cierto que la mujer
Con su amor causa alegría,
Pero cuernos al marido
Le ponen al otro día.
De los que bailan podría
El creer su gusto sincero,
Pero al que brinca en la noche
Ya lo juzgo majadero.
Si por amor al dinero
Al yugo se va un patán,
Seguro que se ha de ver
Como nuestro padre Adán.
No soy afecto á Birján,
La papa nomás me gusta,

Pues de que miro á un soldado,
Solo su mirar me asusta.
Esta reflexión es justa
Pues todo el que piensa bien
Mejor que rifle y pistola,
Oye chillar el sartén.
Mas el tiempo estoy perdiendo
¡Vamos barriguita mía!
[Tentándose el estómago.]
No hay que perder la ocasión
Aprovechemos el día.
Pero antes Sanchito, espía
No venga algún amigote,
Y parte de mi comida
Se trague por el gañote.
*[Vé por todos lados, y no viendo á nin-
guno dice:]*
Tengo un soberbio apetito,
El tiempo hay que aprovechar,
Y ahora que estás tan solito
Ponte, chiquito, á almorzar.
*(Se sienta en el suelo y saca la talega
una servilleta, la extiende entre las
piernas y según va sacando los obje-
tos, dice:*
Venga acá la olla de migas
(Se la pone entre las piernas)
La talega aquí ahora venga,
(Se la pone al frente.)
Y yo comeré gustoso
Lo que todo ella contenga.

ENTRE CONTRATISTAS DE CARNE HUMANA
Disputándose la presa.

108

109

108 Traffickers in Human Flesh. Disputing the Prey. **109** Murder of a Woman.

110

111

110 Daughter Kills Elderly Mother. **111** Female Duel. Two Ladies Challenge Each Other Because their Lovers are Fighting in Cuba on Opposite Sides.

112

113

112 Floating Suicide.
113 Crimes of the Heart.
114 Bloody Drama.
115 Murderer and Suicide.
116 Crime Riddle (Read Tomorrow's Issue).
117 Untitled.
118 Murderer and Suicide.
119 Miser's Death.

114

115

116   Crimen en el misterio. (Léase el número de mañana).

117

118

119

120

121

120 Woman Killing Her Young Children. **121** Another Bejarano. **122** Beastly Cruelty. The Bejarano Family. **123** Exploits of a Child Batterer.
124 Francisco Guerrero, alias the Tailor, Sentenced to Death for Slitting Women's Throats.

123

CRUELDADES FELINAS

122   Las Bajaranos

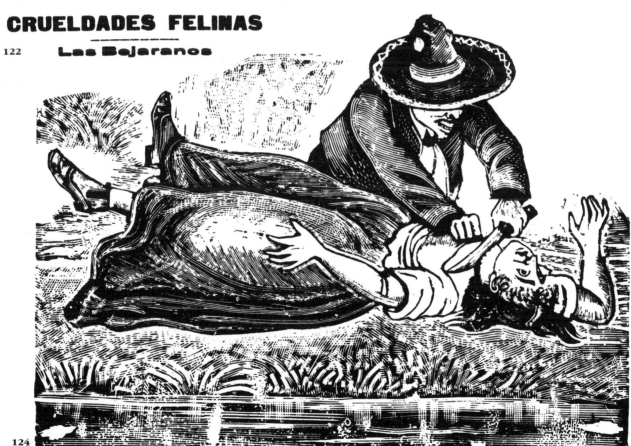

124

Cogida de Rodolfo Gaona

En la Plaza de toros de Puebla, el 13 de Diciembre de 1908.

Veinte centímetros penetró en el cuerpo del diestro el cuerno del toro.

AMARGAS LAMENTACIONES
DE LA AFICION MEXICANA.
Efectos del numero 13.

¿No han de ser supersticiosos
Mirando lo que ha pasado?
Lo que es hoy....ojos llorosos
Traerán los aficionados!

—

Será que el diablo le ayuda
O "de malas," si os parece,
Más por lo visto no hay duda
Que es número malo el 13;
Pues en una misma tarde,
Bueyes mansos, pero arteros,

Con la maña del cobarde,
A los tres buenos toreros
Con que México á contado,
El día trece..... (mala suerte,)
De Diciembre se han mirado
A las puertas de la muerte,
En Celaya, muy ufano,
Luciendo su habilidad
El Reverte Mexicano
Torea con felicidad;
Pero el día 13 llegó
Por obra del mismo pingo,
La de malas que calló
En el merito domingo.

125 Rodolfo Gaona Gored
In Puebla Bullring,
13 December 1908.

94

126
CAUTIONS,
CAVIL AND REGRETS
OF THE SUICIDE
MARIA LUISA NOEKER
FROM BEYOND THE GRAVE

What woes and travails
Hold me here in thrall,
I fancy I still live
And failed to end it all.

Despite the face that the bullet
With deadly fire
Blew my brains to bits,
I did not feel myself expire.

Forever I am condemned
To hold the pistol to my head
In my bedroom, alas,
Not knowing if I am dead.

From my two open wounds
The blood still drips:
One in my head,
The other in the hips.

They tried to grab the gun
But I boldly did cry:
Don't try to stop me
Or I'll blow you sky high.

'Twas shame led me to it
All because of the night
I spent with some bullfighters
Who of my honour made light.

We drained a few glasses
And fun was had by all:
Cirilo Pérez took me
To that cursed dance hall.

I was an admirer of Rodolfo,
The greatest matador of the day,
And went hoping to meet him
Not suspecting foul play.

Now my torments are unending;
I put the gun to my head
Thinking my suffering would be over,
But I took it with me instead.

Sufrimientos, Reflexiones y Consejos de la Suicida

MARIA LUISA NOEKER: EN LA OTRA VIDA.

¡Ay! qué horrible sufrimiento
Tengo en aqueste lugar,
Me figuro que estoy viva,
Que no me pude matar.

Sin embargo que la bala
Certera fué á destrozar
A mi cerebro aturdido
Yo no me sentí acabar.

Aquí me encuentro clavada
En mi cuarto ¡que dolor!
Con la pistola en la mano
Sin saber si vivo ó nó.

Dos heridas me he causado;
Y me mana sangre de ellas:
En la cadera una se halla
Y la otra en la cabeza.

El arma querían quitarme
Pero yo les dije fiera:
Le pego un tiro en el acto
Al que quitármela quiera!

Me suicidé por la honra,
Que en una noche perdí
Por estar con los toreros,
Que se burlaron de mí.

Juntos tomamos licores
Y gozamos sin medida;
Cirilo Perez llevóme
A esa fiesta maldecida;

Yo estaba apasionada,
De Rodolfo el gran torero
Y por conocerlo he ido
Ignorando el plan artero.

Sufro aquí terribles penas
Pues creí con el suicidio
Quitarme padecimientos
Pero al contrario ha salido.

127 Sensational and Harrowing News! A Young Girl throws herself from a Cathedral Tower.

¡SENSACIONAL Y TERRIBLE NOTICIA!

UNA SEÑORITA
que se arroja
DESDE LA TORRE DE CATEDRAL

El día 31 de Mayo del presente año de 1899 y como á las once y treinta minutos de la mañana tuvo efecto el lamentable y terrible acontecimiento que vamos á narrar:

Una bella Señorita Huérfana que contaba veinte años de edad conocida con el nombre de Sofía Ahumada vestida con gran elegancia, subió á las torres de Catedral acompañada del Relojero Bonifacio Mártínez, su ayudante Vicente Estrada y otras dos personas de apellido Aguilar una y la otra Martínez.

Realmente no sabemos que pretestaría la desventurada mujer para lograr subir á aquella prominente altura; pero el caso fué que hallándose dicha Sofía en el seguado piso de la torre que mira al Poniente, se arrojó hacia el suelo con extraordinario y veloz impulso. En el acto y al escuchar el enorme ruido que produjera al caer, agrupóse infinidad de gente de todas clases sociales al lugar donde quedó la mencionada suicida. Dieron parte á la Policía y presentáronse inmediatamente el Sr. Inspector Muñoz acompañado del personal correspondiente. Allí practicáronse las primeras diligencias y lleváronse en una camilla el cadáver á la Inspección que corresponde.

El aspecto que presentaba la joven desdichada era pavoroso y horrible: los ojos saltados completamente de sus órbitas ó lugares, la mandíbula ó quijada inferior quedó fuera de la cavidad de la boca y el cráneo enteramente deshecho y en fragmentos horripilantes. Gran parte de la masa encefálica ó sean los sesos, quedó pendiente en la cornisa del primer piso de la torre, que fué donde chocó el cuerpo fuertemente al venir dando vueltas en el aire cual si fuera esquila ó volantín. Multitud de gente deseosa de contemplar el lugar de tan terrible desgracia, se agrupa, se apiña anhelante en el Atrio de Catedral, comentando cada cual el hecho á su manera y dando su opinión respecto al acontecimiento que tanta y tanta sensación ha causado.

—¿Por qué se mataría? dice uno de tantos.
—¡Pues quién sabe! responde otro.—A poco fué porque su novio le dió calabacitas—¿O tendría acaso alguna deuda?—No; eso no; tan joven y ya con drogas!—Ha de haber sido por su novio!—¡Qué guaje!—¡Pobrecita!—Yo no me suicidaba, poco más ó menos añade una vieja.—Vean vdes, á mí ya va más de seis veces que mi señor me la pega, y ¿qué por eso me he matado? ¡Qué esperanzas! Yo, por taruga.....¿A ver como no me la pega mi marido todos los días!—No, no, dice otro de los curiosos: puede muy bien haber sido esa caída por puro accidente, la desgracia; que ya se le había llegado la raya, porque sólo los guajolotes se mueren la víspera de Corpus. Esa pobre niña tal vez subió inocentemente y sólo por el placer de disfrutar de la hermosa vista que se figuró presentaría la ciudad desde esa altura.—Pero ya vió mucho más que eso.—¡Ya lo creo, ya lo creo! Y así que por este estilo todos hablan y comentan la fatal muerte de la Señorita Ahumada, sin saber realmente la verdad de la causa de semejante desgracia. De todas maneras lo que sí es ciertísimo es que el tal año de 1899 se ha ido presentando desde su principio de lo más feo que pueda haber. Ya se vé, como que en él va á tener lugar el fin del mundo, el día del Juicio Universal. Estos no son más que los preparativos. Suicidios á granel en esta culta Capital, temblores, mucho calor, excediendo al de otros años; quemazones, pestes, homicidios atentados contra la moral nunca vistos como el de Ramón Palma, etc., etc., etc.

En fin, un sinnúmero de calamidades que escandalizan y hacen abrir la boca al más indiferente. Pero ahora el acontecimiento actual es el de la joven Sofía Ahumada, estrellada en el Atrio de Catedral, cuyo acontecimiento es pasto de conversación en todas las casas y grupos de transeúntes por las calles de la ciudad en este día memorable.

MÉXICO.—Imprenta de Antonio Vanegas Arroyo, Calle de Santa Teresa núm. 1.

128 The Suicide.

129 Politics.

POLITICS

130 Emiliano Zapata.

AND NATIONAL EVENTS

Lo que se ve y lo que no se ve.

Fruta del tiempo.

Calabazas para "conserva."

132

133 El último . . . . candidato.

134 **LOS MOSQUETEROS EN EL JURADO.**

131 Now You See It, Now You Don't. (Comment on the lack of justice at the trial of the journalist Ordóñez)

132 This Season's Crop. Add Conservatives and You Get a Pickle.

133 The Latest Candidate.

134 The Musketeers Being Sworn In. Contemporary Celebrities.

135 The Imprisoned Workers address the People,
the Workers, Ladies and Families in Need.
136 The Mexican Broadsheet.
137 Reporters' Notebook (Column heading from Gil Blas).
138 Slippery Customer: Where Education Gets You.

EL FANDANGO

Semanario destinado exclusivamente á la defensa de la clase obrera, decidor de verdade no farolero y sostenedor de cuanto dice en cualquier terreno. No son papas.

Tomo I   México, Martes 27 de Diciembre de 1892.   Núm. 3

LA PRENSA DE A CENTAVO EN MEXICO.

"EL MONITOR DEL PUEBLO."   "GIL BLAS."   "EL FANDANGO."

Uy.. uy.. que le dá el telele,
Acuésten o boca arriba.
—¿Qué es lo que te duele, hijito?
—Ay! padre mio, la barriga.

—No te aflijas, corazón,
Seguro estás indigesto.
—¿Con qué se quitará esto?
—Con un poco de carbón.

Prende lumbre, y al vapor,
Recopila tus noticias,
Saldrán en el «Monitor»
Y no serán escarpicias.

Tú tienes la culpa, hijito,
Con comer bocado ageno,
Que venga pronto un Galeno
De tijera y con su pito;

Y si te esfuerzas tantito
Llegas á resucitar:
¡¡¡Se muere «El Monitorcito»
Ya lo van á confesar!!!

El niño recién nacido
Llegó á ser hombre formal,
A las nubes se ha subido
Y así no la pasa mal.

El pueblo con entusiasmo
Solicita un ejemplar
Para poder deletrear
Y salir de su marasmo.

El camino que ha tomado
Obliga á agarrar el trote,
Cuando dice un remediado:
Chitón, que aquí está el garrote.

Vivimos en un país
De barro y empleomanía,
Y hasta nos dá pulmonía
Cuando se escasea el maíz.

Y que Belén no conozca
Deseamos á «Gil Blasito,»
Allí cualquiera se enrosca
Al dormir en petatito.

Ay Fandango, Fandanguit
FANDANGO del alma mía,
¿Qué pues te pasa, negrit?
—Voy pa la comisaría.

Ya que es tiempo de posadas
Me voy á arrollar al Niño
A Belén, que allá me esperan
Mis valecitos del riño.

—No te metas en hondura
Ni hables de ricos quirósos,
Porque al fin son poderosos
Y matan á tus criatura.

Y encerrado en el tapique
Ni quien se acuerde de ti,
Y lo que siento ¡ay demi!
Que no tomarás tlachpue.

No busques maíz enmazorca
Ni carne en el garabato,
Mira que murió Meléca
Por buscar tres piés l gato.

136

Los obreros presos.

¡AL PUEBLO!

¡A LOS OBREROS!

¡A LAS DAMAS!

Familias en la miseria.

Suscricion abierta por GIL BLAS para auxiliar A LOS IMPRESO RES PRESOS, que actualmente están sufriendo mil penalidades, así como sus familias.

Suma lo colectado hasta el juéves dia 18.	$ 90 05
Un suscritor constante de GIL BLAS.	1 00
V. P.	0 25
Dionisio Rodriguez.	0 50
Srita. María López.	0 50
Felipe Cañas de Iturralde.	2 00
Jesus E. Gutiérrez.	0 50
José M. González y Aguirre.	0 25
Jesus Diaz de Morales.	0 50
Un suscritor de el «Demócra	
Modesto Pérez.	0 25
José Gutiérrez.	0 13
Cayetano Contreras.	0 13
Gregorio Saviñana.	0 12
Nicolás Bravo.	0 12
Félix Rosales.	0 12
Gabriel Paez.	0 12
Leonardo Rodriguez.	0 12
Cecilio Camarena.	0 12
José María Rodriguez.	0 12
Pablo Vargas.	0 18
Isidro Hernández.	0 06
Gregorio Cibrian.	0 06
Vicente Sánchez.	0 06
Víctor Peez.	0 06
Román Ortiz.	0 06
Aureliano Esquivel.	0 06

CARNET DE REPORTERS

A última hora hemos sabido qu

137

UN CULEBRON

NOTICIOSO

A lo que llegan los hombres por sus letras

139

140

141

139 Amador Salazar.
140 The Tiger of Santa Julia.
141 Death of a Revolutionary.
142 Emilian o Zapata.
143 Ballad of Macario Romero.
144 Ballad of Heraclio Bernal.

ZAPATA.

142

143

144

105

145

145 Ballad of the Nickle
Rout.
146 Ballad of the 20 Cents
Victory.
147 Gil Blas Masthead
148 After All That Crowing.

146

GIL BLAS

PERIÓDICO JOCO — SERIO ILUSTRADO

Segunda época. | México, Sábado 30 de Mayo de 1896. | Número 1112.

147

LA INSULITA DE D. TEODOLITO.

149

LA DEMOCRACIA EN HIDALGO.

¡VIVA LA LIBERTAD!

150

149 Don Teodolito's Little Island (Criticism of the Governor of Veracruz for ineffectiveness)

150 Democracy in Hidalgo. (Cartoon on the Governor of the State of Hidalgo, for obstructing the sale of certain newspapers.)

151 Croupiers, Gamblers and the People.

152 One Dies and Another is Born. New Year Allegory.

153 Tonche, Give Us a Break... (Comment on political affairs in the state of Guerrero.)

151

152

Año nuevo.....

153

154

154   Tasty food. Uncle Sam consuming Cuba.
155   The Anguish of the Press.
156   Keep It Up, Comrades!
157   Antique Dealer.
        No Doubt about it;
        It's got to be the God of . . . Kidney Beans.
158   Fraternal Stew.
159   Plan for a Monument to the People.

Congojas del Gran Rotativo.

155

156

UN ANTICUARIO.

—No, no hay duda; este debe de ser el dios de los....frijoles

157

«GIL BLAS» va á hacer un guisote
de amigos del amigote,
para dárselo á comer,
en el próximo mitote
que á Mena le van á hacer.
Ese va á ser un banquete

158

Proyecto de un monu-
mento al pueblo

159

La risa del pueblo mexicano.

161 Clock Tower.

GACETA CALLEJERA.

Esta hoja volante se publicará cuando los acontecimientos de sensación lo requieran.

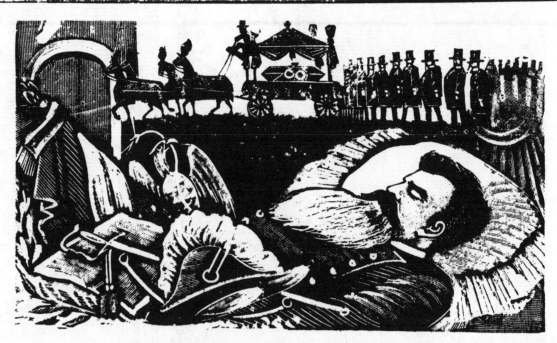

LLEGADA DEL CADAVER
Del C. General
MANUEL GONZALEZ
A ESTA CAPITAL.

162 Arrival in the Capital of the Body of Commander-in-Chief General Manuel Gonzalez.

163 Sad News. Much Lamented Death of the Illustrious General and Federal State Governor, Señor José Ceballos.

Desde las tres de la tarde de ayer, 9 de Mayo se agrupaba en la estación de San Lázaro un inmenso número de ciudadanos,

El carro fúnebre en que lo trajeron es de aspecto imponente, y sencillo. La caja es de lo más elegante que habia en todo Méji-

La capa tiene muy buenas molduras, y un cristal en toda la longitud del féretro que permite ver el cadáver perfectamente bien.

162

GACETA CALLEJERA.

Esta hoja volante se publicará cuando los acontecimientos de sensación lo requieran.

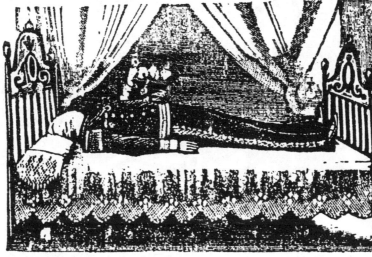

EL CADÁVER ENBALSAMADO.

Sentida muerte del ilustrado General y Gobernador del Distrito Federal Señor

JOSE CEBALLOS.

Una pulmonia fulminante en muy corto tiempo vino á dar término á su existencia.

Hoy Miércoles 19 del corriente á las cuatro y media de la mañana falleció en su casa Paseo de la Reforma núm. 4. Desde estos momentos su familia, las calles adyacentes,

A toda clase de solicitudes de las tres categorías, es decir, la alta, la media, y la ínfima, las recibía con la misma dulzura y cordialidad.

Nunca se le veía de mal humor, y si lo tenia, procuraba reprimirlo ante sus visitadores

163

¡CASO RARO

UNA MUJER QUE DIO A LUZ TRES NIÑOS
Y CUATRO ANIMALES.

164 Rare Case! A Woman Gives Birth to Three Children and Four Animals.

RARE

Un caso de hidrofobia.

165 A case of Hydrophobia (fear of water).

CASES

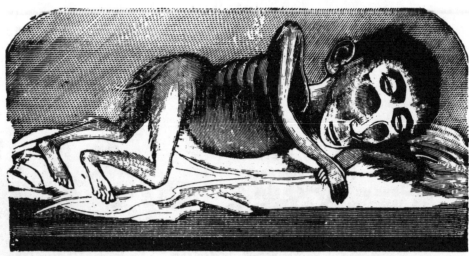

166

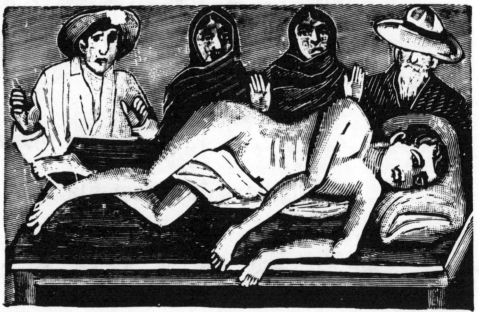

167

166 Freak.
167 Freak with Legs instead of Arms.
168 Amazing Freak! Pig with Face of a
    Man, Eyes of a Fish, and Horn on
    its Forehead.

¡Extraño y nunca visto acontecimiento!

UN CERDO CON CARA DE HOMBRE

OJOS DE PESCADO
Y UN CUERNO EN. LA FRENTE

A principios del mes de Junio próximo pasado, se vió en Guásima. mineral perteneciente a Sinaloa el fenómeno más singular que haya producido la naturaleza.

Una cerda dió a luz el rarísimo ser que tanto llama la atención, el cual consiste en un marrano monstruoso, pues tiene la piel de la misma calidad y color del pellejo humano; las manos, patas y pezuñas son de cerdo verdaderamente, lo mismo que la cola, bastante corta; pero todo esto es en cuanto a la figura y organización únicamente. En la barriga se le ven dos hileras de tetas y el cordón umbilical. La parte que corresponde al tronco se asemeja al de un hombre; la cabeza es muy perfecta y está cubierta de cabello grueso, sin ser cerdas todavía; las orejas son exactísimas a las de la gente y colocadas en perfecta posición humana; en cada carrillo o cachete tiene un lunar de pelo; el hocico presenta una hermosa dentadura de gente también; la nariz y barba están semi-cubiertos con algunos bellos ásperos; los ojos se ven unidos y sumamente redondos, no siendo de cerdo ni de hombre, pues más bien semejan ser de pescado; sobre cada uno de estos ojos forma arco la ceja y en la parte más alta, es decir, en la frente, luce un regular cuerno o trompa adornada con pocos bellos. La persona que tiene en su poder este

singularísimo y jamás visto fenómeno, es D. Agustín Castro, muy conocido en la ciudad de Pánuco.

Este señor, como decimos, conserva el hombre cerdo muerto naturalmente y en una vasija con alcohol, causando a todos los que lo ven la consiguiente admiración y asombro.

No cabe duda que cada día se miran semejantes casos de lo mas raro que pueda uno imaginarse, pero a éstos no se les dá más solución por ahora que la naturaleza caprichosa. pues darle otra, sería pensar muy mal respecto a la humanidad

169 Siamese Twins

170 Incredible Case of the Woman Who Split in Two and Turned into a Snake and a Ball of Fire!

171 Child with Face on its Buttocks.

172 Man with a Small Leg Protruding from His Ribs.

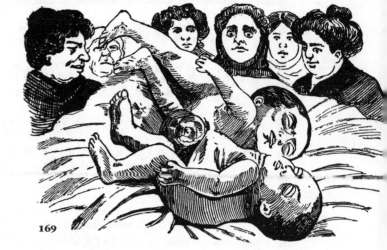

169

SUCESO NUNCA VISTO

¡¡Una mujer que se divide en dos mitades, convirtiéndose en serpiente y en esfera de fuego!!

170

171

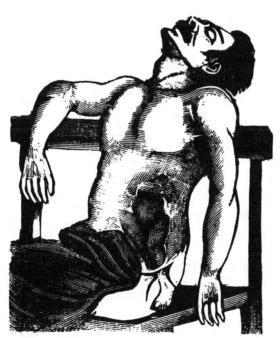

172

CALAVERAS

173, 174 Posada vignettes from the French language magazine *Le Petit Gaulois*.

MEXICO-MACABRE.

CIMETIÈRE

DU "PETIT GAULOIS"

2 NOVEMBRE 1897

A l'occasion

DU

2 NOVEMBRE,

Nous

PUBLIERONS

Un Numéro Spécial

HILARANT, RIGOUILLARD ET DIGESTIF.

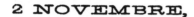

AU TIVOLI DE***.

—

ÉPILOGUE DU DERNIER BANQUET.

LE CARNAVAL A MEXICO

—

La rédaction du "Petit Gaulois" au bal masqué.

UN ORPHÉON EXOTIQUE.

Ce bon Chambon.

—

175   124

CALAVERAS!!!

CALAVERAS!!!

MEXICO-MACABRE.

CIMETIÈRE DU PETIT GAULOIS

2 NOVEMBRE 1887

A l'occasion

DU

2 NOVEMBRE,

Nous

PUBLIERONS

Un Numéro Spécial

HILARANT, RIGOUILLARD ET DIGESTIF.

Qu'on se le dise!!!

Prix d'une annonce illustrée:

DEUX PIASTRES

LE FOSSOYEUR-EN-CHEF:

Cocorico.

MEXICO-MACABRE.

CIMETIÈRE

DU "PETIT GAULOIS"

2 NOVEMBRE 1887

A l'occasion

DU

2 NOVEMBRE,

Nous

PUBLIERONS

Un Numéro Spécial

HILARANT, RIGOUILLARD ET DIGESTIF.

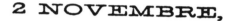

Qu'on se le dise!!!

Prix d'une annonce illustrée:

DEUX PIASTRES

LE FOSSOYEUR-EN-CHEF:

Cocorico.

IMPRENTA ECONÓMICA, CINCO DE MAYO. 22.

Read all about the Pantheon of Lovers,
Mortals who live in this vale of tears,
And in the silence of the tomb
You'll find all manner of joys and fears.

Here are two skeletons
Parading without shame:
In this life she was Dolores
And Contreras was his name

Here lies a brave toreador
Who died of distress,
Booed by the public
For always making a mess;
A butt in the backside
Took him to the land of the blessed.
And when he got there
He was such a blockhead
That thinking they were bulls
He started to fight the dead.

This brilliant general
Won a thousand battles,
The only one he lost
Was with death's rattle.
Now you can't tell
Whether he's a genius or a nit,
Today on a skull
His general's hat does sit,
And despite all his medals
he's changed quite a bit.

This fancy couple here
Are birds of a feather;
They did not marry for love
But see how they stride out together.

'Are you game for love?'
'That depends on the price and the day.'
'Can I take you to Dolores' place?'
'OK cowboy, right away!'

'Come now, don't be so jealous.'
'You think I've got no eyes in my head.'
'If anyone plays Romeo to me
He can count himself dead.'

'I want no more of your love!'
'I've been faithful and true!'
'Revolting skeleton, leave me alone,
I want to be rid of you.'

And the jealous cowboy
Finally rose to the bait,
And went off to the grave
To mourn his mate.

'Drown your sorrows.'
'Have another one on me.'
'OK, but what's the hurry?'
'We're off Dolores to see.'

A fairer lass
I never did see
In the whole of Japan
Or the China Sea,
She sang with such grace
Tra-la-la tra-la-lee;
No one sang a song
Of love so sweet
As the girl at Dolores' place
Who by a grave I did meet.

Don't throw a dead rat
Into my vault,
That crafty old skeleton
Has got his eyes on the door-bolt;
My skull is not blind,
And if loud I do sing
Today is the last time,
For soon Death's sting
Will dispose of my remains
And my skeleton will be nothing.

'If I can do penance
With you, my fair dame,
Then for the grave
I am ready and game.'

177 The Great Pantheon of Lovers.

EL GRAN PANTEON AMOROSO.

Leed, pues, este Panteón de los Amores   Y hallaréis muchos gustos y dolores
Todos los que habitáis aquí en la tierra,   Que el gran secreto de la tumba encierra.

Aquí yace un buen torero,
Que murió de la aflicción
De ser mal banderillero,
Silbado en cada función;
Ha muerto de un revolcón
Que recibió en la trasera,
Y era tanta su tontera
Que en el sepulcro ya estaba
Y á los muertos los toreaba
Convertido en calavera.

General que fué de suerte
Y mil acciones ganó
Y sólo una la perdió
La que tuvo con la muerte;
Nadie hay que al mirarle acierte
Si fué un sabio ó de tontera,
Hoy es una calavera
Con gorro en verdad montado,
Y aunque esté condecorado
Hoy ya no es lo que antes era.

Aquí van con sus amores
Gozando dos calaveras:
La que en vida fué Dolores,
Y él de apellido Contreras.

Aquí tienen á dos muertos,
Tal cual para cada quien,
Casados por desaciertos,
Paseando y vistiendo bien.

—¿Usted no sabe de amores?
—A según cuando conviene.
—¿Quiere ir conmigo á Dolores?
—Charrito, si aquí me tiene.

—Adios; no ande de celoso,
—Me cree con los ojos tuertos.
—Si alguno me hiciera el oso
Se contaba entre los muertos.

—No quiero más amistad.
—Mi amor no ha sido quimera.
—Dejadme en la soledad
Y en paz, torpe calavera.

Y aquel charrito celoso
Pudo al fin tragar el queso,
Y con su muerte afanoso
Marchóse á llorar el hueso.

—Métale á la penca, vale.
—Atórele á los ardores.
—Ojas; pero no me jale.
—Pos vamos para Dolores.

No he visto mujer más fina
Pa cantar una canción
Ni en toditito el Japón
Ni en todita la China,
Pues canta la muy indina
Con tal aire y tal sal salero,
Que no hay en el mundo entero
Quien cante bien sus amores
Como ésta que ví en Dolores
Junto á un sepulcro ratero.

No me eche una rata muerta
Vestida de colorado,
El muerto chino taimado
Que me ha espiado ya la puerta;
Mi calavera no es tuerta,
Y si cantó sin quimera
Es hoy por la vez postrera,
Pues pronto la muerte flaca
Ya mero mis restos saca
Y á Dios de mi calavera.

—Con tal de llorar el hueso
Con usted, preciosa güera,
Me va á dar pa copa y queso
Por muerto y por calavera.

México.—Imprenta de Antonio Vanegas Arroyo, Calle de Santa Teresa número 1.

CALAVERA DE LAS ARTES

Sin pretensión de pobre ni de rica,
Aquí donde me ven valgo una chica.

Se acabaron por fin los artesanos,
Que hoy saludan á todos sus hermanos

Pobres de los carpinteros
Que con el puro cepillo,
Al cedro le sacan brillo
Y al marchante los dineros.
    Ahora en el panteón están
Aserrando duro y fuerte,
Para enterrar á la muerte
En un lujoso cajón.
    Se les acabó la busca
De las chambas por su cuenta.
Que hasta el mejor se amedrenta
Cuando la muerte se ofusca.

    Los sastres aquí están secos
Como mulas de alquiler,
Pues ya no pueden hacer
Como antes tantos *chalecos*.
    Ya no se podrán robar
Los pedacitos de paño,
Que aquí no cabe el engaño
Ni hay modo de cercenar.
    Ellos que eran encargados
De vestir á los demás,
Andaban todos cual más
Enteramente encuerados.
    Y por la misma razón
Hoy condenados están,
A hacerle al diablo un gabán,
Un saco y un pantalón.

    Aquí están los zapateros
Tan alegres y bromistas,
Le jalan recio á las pitas
Y masetean á los cueros.
    Ellos que arman el mitote
Echándola de valientes,
Son ahora los más prudentes
Porque les entró el *cerote*.
    Con la muerte aquí no juegan
Y por eso están contritos,
Y llorarán sus delitos
De los cuales hoy reniegan.

Los talabarteros pillos
Que tuvieron buena suerte,
Le están bordando á la muerte
Cantinas y báquerillos.
    Y aunque ya son calaveras
Las medidas no rebusan,
Y aún allá en el panteón usan
Su leznita y sus tijeras.
    Los finchados sombrereros
Que hasta se escupen la mano
Planchando un rico *jarano*
Para los buenos rancheros,
    Más lucen su habilidad.
En tratando con los muertos
Pues entónces están ciertos
De ir hasta la eternidad.
    Y siendo ya calaveras
También las ribeteadoras,
Se pasarán buenas horas
Siendo amigotes de veras.

Los enamorados *patos*
Que embadurnan las esquinas
Y enamoran las catrinas
Pasando así dulces ratos,
    Cuando vayan al panteón
Su trabajo han de tener.
Pues ellos le han de poner
Su nombre á cada cajón.
    Ya no echarán sus jalones
Del tlamapa rico y puro;
Ya no ganarán ni un duro
Por pintar los jacalones
    Ya no se irán con las gatas
Á pasear en Todos Santos,
Pues van á los Camposantos
Que hasta les vuelan las patas.
    Los bizcocheros mugrientos
Que andan de la harina en torno,
Harán allá entre los muertos
Calaveritas al horno.

Los impresores de oficio
Que *maton el sapo* tanto,
e van todos haciendo *equis*
amino del Camposanto.
    Y allí á San Lúnes le rezan
Llenos de fé y contrición,
Pues no olvidan que este Santo
Fue en el mundo su patrón
    Y aunque ya sean esqueletos
Resecos y apolillados,
Todavía se la han de echar
De pillos y enamorados.

Los buenos bojalateros
Que la echan de cosa fina,
Diciendo que no hay como ello
Para hacer bien una tina,
    Al hacer la gran pirueta
Verán con dolor profundo,
Que el orgullo nada vale
Como nada vale el mundo.
    Se acabaron los faroles
Y las jaulas de pericos,
Ya no harán recojedores
Ni coches para los chicos.
    Aquellos de Michoacán
Que á México están viniendo,
Para el panteón se irán yendo
Y ya de allí no saldrán.

    Ya el mamonero no canta
Estando allá en el panteón,
omo aquí en Semana Santa:
Dos rosquillas y un mamón.
    Y en fin, marcharán en bola
Y sin guardar distinción,
Toditos los artesanos
Con rumbo para el panteón.
    Y después de tanta facha
Y de tantas peloteras,
Serán todos un mentón
De peladas calaveras.

Propiedad particular.—Imprenta de Antonio Vanegas Arroyo Calle de Santa Teresa. número 1.—México

178 Calavera of the Arts.
I make no claim to rhythm or rhyme
But to my customers I'm worth a
dime
The artisans have met their end,
And today come back to greet their
friends.

179 Calavera of the Revolutionary.

180 Calavera of Soldier from Oaxaca. **181** Revolutionary Calavera. **182** Skeletons' Fiesta in the Porfirio Diaz Park.

.....GRAN.....
VERBENA DE CALAVERAS
EN EL PARQUE PORFIRIO DIAZ.

CERA. PURA.

El Parque Porfirio Diaz
El mero dia de finados,
Estará de rechupete
Como jamás se ha mirado.
Gran verbena se prepara
Un lucido verbenazo
Donde serán calaveras
Toditos; pues ¡esta claro!
Verbena de calaveras,
Alegrona por demás,
Como ninguna se ha visto
Ni se habrá visto jamás.
Los panteones, desde luego
Sin un muerto quedarán,
Porque todos irán listos
A la gangota ¡caray!
¡Cuanto puesto! ¡canillones!
Fruta y dulces sin contar,
Chacualole, pan de muerto,
Golletes, al por millar;
Magnifica barbacoa
Cacahuates....y la mar!
Sobre todo, mucha penca,
Curado como no hay más,
Que solo al verlo se trepa
Sin poderlo remediar.
Y respecto á diversiones;
Ninguna les faltará,

Esqueletos maromeros
Darán el salto mortal,
Y titeres y columpios,
Por todas partes habrá.
Varias músicas alegres
Buenas piezas tocarán
Con instrumentos de huesos
Y toditos bailarán
Patas arriba y sentados
Marcha fúnebre y cancán.
Aquello va á estar muy bueno
Magnífico, sin rival.
Es el gran dia de jolgorio
Que los muertos se darán,
Pues solo cada año comen
Y vuelo al hilacho dán.
El atracón será magno
Y la borrachera más,
Y habrá muchachas reguapas

¡Pues vaya si las habrá!
Con caras de calavera
Simpáticas por demás,
Todas pelando los dientes
Y prontas para bailar.
Novios habrá por montones,
Que en esto de enamorar,
Los muertos son muy picudos
Y habladores sin igual.
Las cuestiones y los pleitos
Vendrán como es natural,
Y allá van los canillazos
¡Y trompones pum! pum! prás!
Y aquello será un rebumbio
Del mísmito Satanás.
Por aquí corre un esqueleto
Sin quijadas ¡¡ay!! ay!! ay!!
Por allá otro sin brazos,
Sin calavera los más......
Unos chillan, otros ladrán...
Résumen de lo ocurrido:
No se vayan á espantar:
Todos los muertos se mueren
Y aquí gloria y después paz.
Así se acaba el festejo
Y ya no hay más de que hablar....
Un responso y una cera
Y que les vaya muy ...mal!

LAS BICICLETAS.

Calaveras of cyclists,
Sportsmen and aviators bold,
Of motorists young
And tram-drivers old.

Stand clear, make way
For the messengers of doom!
They spare none they encounter
So leave them plenty of room.

Pull out the throttle,
Give it all it's got,
There's no stopping these skeletons
Who go like a shot.
Serving girls, look out,
Keep the tram-lines clear,
Or of you they'll make
Blancmange, I fear,
And wigs on your bald pates
You will have to wear.

No one can pip
Death on wheels at the post,
I'm prepared to make a bet
With whoever offers the most.
Let's clear out of the way
Without further ado,
Or there'll be nothing left standing
By the time you're through,
And if you're not careful
There'll be nothing left of you.

Watch out for the motorists
Because everyone knows
That he who gets in their path
At risk of life and limb goes.
And like it or not
It's off to the grave,
There'll be not a soul left
Mankind to save,
For all will be swept away
As if by a tidal wave.

The bootblacks may run
For their lives and gulp,
But the paper-boys
Will be turned to pulp.
And the candy-sellers
Will share their fate,
For the time has come
For merriment to abate
And it's off to the graveyard
Without further wait.

The countryman and
The city-dweller

Down the road to death
Must travel together.

Death will order the dealers
From El Volador who peddle
To get on their bike
Before they can meddle;

From the Calle de Plateros
The dandies and beaus
Will decamp to the cemetery
To swank and pose.

For if there are traitors
Who kiss the foreigner's hand,
There will always be Mexicans
To defend their land.

Muttering their prayers,
The devout old crones
In a whited sepulchre
Will deposit their bones.

With their secondhand books
And their rusty scrap iron,
They'll go off to join the skeletons
No matter how much they whine.

The Hercules who in the bars
Get into a brawl
In the lonely graveyard
With maggots will crawl.

So, Gringos, look out
For the cyclists so fleet;
If you get in their way
They will make you mincemeat.

Here come the cyclists!
Gentlemen, make way!
It's the aviators' and motorists'
And tram-drivers' day!

The market-vendors of San Juan
Who their customers cheat
The day after tomorrow
For the maggots will be meat.

Death has made off
With the poor politicians
For tampering with
Other people's acquisitions.

The doctors for all their science
Will never overcome Death's power
But they too will march
To the grave in their hour.

Neither typhoon at sea
Nor on land tornado
Can cause as much havoc
And as many deaths as they do.

All the fishmongers
Whose goods are rotten
Will go straight to Hell
To expiate their gains ill-gotten.

As a result of their intrigues
Their money they did lose,
And now they are broke
And have got the blues.

The lawyers, despite
Their jurisprudence and cunning,
From the cyclists' wrath
Will find themselves running,

The brakes have failed,
They're out of control,
And Death is waiting
To take its toll.

The brazen young hussies
Who strut without care
Will be skeletons whose charms
Are truly laid bare.

They say the Yanks
Are bent on conquest,
But the skeletons here
Will not let them rest;

And with the judges and clerks
Piled up in a heap
They too with the maggots
Company will keep.

But they'll be back next year,
Mercilessly running down
All who come near.

183 The Cyclists.

LAS BICICLETAS.

Calaveras de ciclistas,
de sportmen y de aviadores,
de jóvenes motoristas
y de viejos conductores.

.bran paso, que aquí van
los ciclistas de la muerte
atropellan al que encuentran
porque así sería su suerte.

Apránla, que lleva bala
y ahora sí que vá deveras,
que no hay quien les dé garrote
a estas lindas calaveras.
Cuidense las garbanceras
de no ponerse en los rieles,
que en masa de pasteles
se quedarán convertidas,
y las feas y presumidas
se peinarán de caireles.

A la muerte en bicicleta
nadie gana en la carrera,
y le apuesta al mas pintado
aquí mismo y en donde quiera.
Vámonos echando fuera
sin hacerse del rogar,
porque no van a dejar
ni un titere con cabeza,
y no ha de haber entereza
que no sepan quebrantar.

Ojo con los *mataristas*
porque es cosa bien sabida,
que el que se les pone enfrente
se despide de la vida.
Y el que quiera mas que pida
pues se van para el panteón
y no quedará un pelón
para semilla en el mundo,
pues como viento iracundo
matarán sin ton ni son.

Aunque chillen y aunque corran
los bulliciosos boleros,
se harán una pepitoria
con los chicos papeleros.
Los pobres charamusqueros
les han de hacer compañia,
porque se ha llegado el día
de que le lloren al hueso
y que calme el exceso
de su constante alegría.

Lo mismo el campesino que el hombre de la ciudad, por la senda de la muerte al fin tendrán que rodar.

Los viejos del volador
volarán como aereoplanos,
sin que la muerte les deje
tiempo de meter las manos.
Se irán con sus libros viejos
y sus mohosos fierritos,
en parranda de esqueletos
sin que les valgan sus gritos.
Las fruteras de San Juan
que dán tan caras las peras,
pronto se convertirán
en poladas calaveras.
Los que en todos los mercados
venden pescados podridos
irán derecho al infierno
por no estar arrepentidos.
No escaparán de *pelarse
de casquete* y muy de veras,
las coquetas relamidas
pretenciosas calaveras

Los orgullosos catrines
de la calle de Plateros,
se irán a lagartijear
por todos los cementerios.
Los Hércules que a trompadas
hacen gala en los salones,
serán pasto de gusanos
en los desiertos panteones.
A los pobres diputados
se los llevó la pelona,
por meterse en la camisa
de once varas y de lona.
Por meterse a conspirar
perdieron quinientos duros,
y se hallan acongojados
metidos en mil apuros.
Aunque dicen que los yankis
vienen en son de conquista,
lo que es con estas pelonas
no se han de acabar ni chica.

Que si hay malos mexicanos
que ayuden al extranjero,
siempre sobrarán patriotas
que defiendan este suelo.
Y que se cuiden los gringos
de estos ágiles ciclistas,
que si los hallan al paso
les van a sacar las tripas.
Los médicos con su ciencia
no van a encontrar la cura,
y marchando por delante
camino a la sepultura.
Los abogados, con ser
tan hábiles y juristas,
no lograrán escapar
de la ira de estos ciclistas.
Y formando una pelota
con los jueces y escribanos
irán a servir de pasto
a los inmundos gusanos.

Las viejitas mogigatas
mascullando sus rosarios,
irán a dar con sus huesos
en los desiertos osarios.
¡Abran camino, señores!
que aquí van estos ciclistas;
aviadores, motoristas
y valientes conductores.
Ni las trombas de los mares,
ni el huracán del desierto,
han de causar tantos males
ni han de dejar tanto muerto.
Que ya perdieron los frenos
y el garrote no funciona,
y nadie se ha de escapar
del poder de la pelona.
Ya se ván estos ciclistas
y vendrán el año entrante,
y atropellarán sin tregua
a quien se ponga delante.

Imprenta de Antonio Vanegas Arroyo, 2a. Santa Teresa 43. México. 1913

184

185

186

"Calaveras de Coyotes y Meseras"·

Un gato del otro mundo
me escribe en «cuero» de gente
(pergamino el más decente
que usan por su ignoto rumbo),
las quejas que aquí transcribo,
no es fuerza raspar con lija,
por lo «rebién» redactadas!

Son quejas a viento dadas
que nadie tomará en cuenta,
pero serán publicadas
en esta excelente imprenta,
y del vulgo conocidas:
¡Olvidos del mundo afrenta,
negruras de ciertas vidas!
¿Y qué nos importa ahora
seriedad tan inoportuna?
¡Venga ya charla sonora
de filosofía gatuna!

El «difunto muerto» gato
se queja de las meseras,
las más guapa· calaveras
que saben pasar el rato

Les han quitado la chamba
a monos y cantineros,
pues los clientes parrancheros
que entra un danzón, y la «rumba»
se beben litros enteros
de Mocte... ma ... chalaba

o de barril, de Toluca,
y al gachupín dando ·laba·
arman terrible borona,
y ya cuando están bien chispos
se meten al ·reservado·
y rezan el ·ba---avado·
como rezan los obispos:
·haciendo los ojos bizcos
y el capuchón remangado.·

Y las ladinas meseras
estafan a los ñis,
bebiéndoselas de anís
para no ser calaveras.

Por eso, por trapacheras,
por ponerse así las botas,
por lias y descaradotas
se han de·volver calaveras.

No que hasta en las neverías
hacen sus vaciloncitos,
y sus grandes porquerías
allá en los reservaditos ...

¡Puercas, cochinas, grotescas,
se han de·volver calaveras

por andar en la verbena!
—(¡Quién tuviera una docena
para este tiempo de frío!)

Ahora, mis lectores ·píos,·
a un asunto diferente,
hablemos ya de otra gente
que igualmente os interesa,
como dijo Juan de Tolas:
—¡Si no os tocan la cabeza,
al ménos os echan Bolsa.·

¡Oh la Bolsa! ¡los coyotes!
¡Manos arriba, señores,
que allá viene, dado a trotes
el jefe de estafadores!

—¡Compro dollar, infalibles!
—¡Cambio aztecas por morralla!
—¡Oiga, señor no se vaya,
los otros son más terribles!
—¡Compro pesos y toulones!
—¡Vendo dollar, compro Banco!
—¡Mira esos payos .... juilones,
a esos sí me los atranco!

Y era un escándalo atroz,
no dejaban transitar;
nadie dejaban pasar
al dirigirle la voz....
¡Ah, coyotes tan .... molones,
por tantas tracalas fieras,

todos serán calaveras,
enterrados sin calzones!
Les dieron su "contra-coba,"
como a la peste bubónica,
y de Isabel la Católica
los barrieron con escoba....
Perdieron sus "negocitos"
que hacían a lo descarado;
conozco yo coyotitos
que se las echan de lado:
No daban su día por ménos
de doce a quince murlacas,
¡y cuando los días son buenos!
¡y cuando abundan los necos!
menudean los papanatas
y "tupen recio" los "jinchos"
¡qué juergas, qué serenatas
qué parrandas, qué borchichos!
¡Ah, muchachos calaveras!
¡Calaveras!, (¡y en vida!,
la muerte no se descuida
y a las gentes parranderas,
que gustan de las meseras
y del ·Lonch· en reservado,
¡calaveras, calaveras!
serán del morrongo airado;
que con el rabo parado
les darán su pasaporte
escogiendo calaveras....
¡Y entierra a cada coyote
con "Siento siete meseras"!

CENFORM .... Imp. Vanegas Arroyo, —Sta. Teresa 10.—México, D. F.   CINCO CENTAVOS

187

La Calavera del Tenorio
De la Colonia de la Bolsa.
ojo, mucho ojo, señores | Que aquí esta la calavera
Del mismo don Juan Tenorio
Que no le teme a cualquiera.

En el barrio de la Bolsa
No hay que echarla de Tenorio,
Porque allí se deja el cuera
Y se vá uno al Purgatorio.

Porque allí hasta las mujeres,
sin miedo a ser calaveras,
son tan bravas que parecen
unas positivas fieras.

María La Boña, que es guapa,
de su valor hace gala
y no le meten cerote
ni con puñal, ni con bala.

Ella tiene su querido
y ninguno se le acerca,
pues a cualquiera le dice:
—¿Qué le gusta? ¿Me lo merca?

Pues eche fuera la «punta»
que es la moneda que gasto,
que aquí tengo para darle
para sus puercos a pasto.·

Y para ella no hay Tenorios,
ni muertos, ni calaveras,
que se atora a chavetazos
con el mismito Juan Cuerdas.

Si vienen los zapatistas
a invadir el territorio,
no hay temores; que aquí está
el bravo Don Juan Tenorio.

Y el que quiera hacer la prueba
no más que se ponga avispa,
que si escapa de Don Juan
a Don Luis no se le chispa

Don Juan viene decidido
a limpiar la población,
de los malos comerciantes
que roban sin ton ni son.

Por eso ha de despachar
sin piedad ni miramientos,
a los que tanto encarecen
los primeros alimentos.

Viene a defender al pobre,
víctima de la avaricia,
y al que no quede contento
le hará sangrienta caricia.

Alerta, pues, comerciantes,
y no rompan la cobija,
que para ganar la plata
y quedarse sin un hueso.

Consideren a los pobres
que para ganar un peso,
tienen que echar media vida
y quedarse sin un hueso.

No se fien de la guaracha,
pues también se han de morir,
y cuando aprieten los dientes
el diablo se ha de reir.

Que todos se han de volver
calaveras corrompidas
y las más avariciosas
serán las más corrompidas.

Prevénganse los famosos
valedores de la Palma,
a ver si hay uno que quiera
conmigo romperse el alma.

Ya se pueden prevenir
los bravos de Tomatlán,
por si hay alguno que quiera
que le dé gordas Don Juan.

San Antonio Tomatlán
que es barrio de los malhora,
a ver si hay uno que diga
que con Tenorio se atora.

Vengan aquí de Jamaica
los planchadores curtidores,
y verán lo que es canela
y no de los alfajores.

Cuídense de Juan Tenorio
que viene con muchas ganas,
de abotonarles de duro
las purititas badanas.

Que si hoy calavera soy
ayer indomable fuí,
y no se olviden que estoy
esperándolos aquí.

Y vengan los de San Cosme,
los del barrio de Nonoalco,
que para mí son muy pocos
en cuanto mi espada saco.

Esos de San Sebastián
que se las dan de maldito,
conmigo no valen papas
ni me espantan con sus gritos.

Y al que me pida la gorda
se la daré martajada,
que a mí no me asustan cocos
ni con la cara tapada.

No necesito pregones
pues mi valor es notorio,
y esto que escribo, lo firmo
con mi nombre: Juan Tenorio.

Los pobres no toman leche
porque se halla por las nubes,
y el neutle, sólo lo beben
en el cielo, los querubes.

El pan ya lo están vendiendo
del grueso de unas obleas,
y las tortillas no pueden
comerse de puro feas.

No olviden los comerciantes
que aquí está Don Juan Tenorio,
capaz de hacer con sus tripas
el más perfecto jolgorio.

No es de la Colonia Roma
no me importa que sean gringos,
pues ya verán que conmigo
no importa que den respingo.

Los valientes de Tepito
tienen que ponerse changos,
que aquí está Don Juan Tenorio
que no les hará bailar tangos.

Imprenta de Antonio Vanegas Arroyo, 2a. Santa Teresa 43. -- México, 1913.

188

---

184 *Calaveras employed to serve*
who will get what they deserve.

185 *Here comes the skeleton*
From his peregrinations
To join in the fun
At the centenary celebrations.

186 Detail from the Calavera of Cupid

187 Calaveras of wheeler-dealers
(popularly known as 'coyotes')
and barmaids.

188 Calavera of the Stock Exchange Don Juan.
Gentlemen be on your guard,
For the Calavera here
Is Don Juan Tenorio in person,
Who knows no respect or fear.

190

191

192

189 Chin Chun Chan.
190 *(Calavera Catrina)*
     Calavera of Society Belle.
     Fun-loving Calaveras.
     Today's maids in their Sunday best
     Tomorrow will be skeletons laid to rest.
191 Calavera of Chorus-Girl.
192 Calavera with Top Hat and Cigar.

EL PURGATORIO ARTISTICO
EN EL QUE YACEN LAS CALAVERAS
De los Artistas y Artesanos.

En este Purgatorio sin segundo Los artistas se ven de todo el mundo.

He aquí el cuadro que nos representa palpablemente lo que es el principio de la vida y lo que es su inexorable fin. —"Hoy por tí y mañana por mí."

 Cobijados están por un sudario
Artesanos y artistas á millares,

 Y es seguro hallarás al que buscares
Por orden singular de abecedario.

AGUSTINILLO EL ALBAÑIL

Tú fuiste un buen albañil,
Cargaste sobre tus hombros
Los adoves, los escombros
Con dificultades mil.
Pusiste el tejamanil
Con una destreza rara,
Cargaste con tu cuchara
Al pasar á la otra vida,
Y hoy tu cara es convertida
En calavera muy rara.

CARPINTERO DE AFICION.

Tú hiciste muchos primores,
Como fueron malas puertas
Unas torcidas ó tuertas
Y otros malos mostradores.
Pero en fin, tus valedores
Que te quisieron de veras,
Vienen todos con sus ceras
Y muy piadosos á verte,
Que estás por tu infausta suerte
Entre tantas calaveras.

ENCUADERNADOR DE FAMA.

Una biblioteca entera
A un doctor encuadernaste,
Y con él muy bien quedaste
Con obra tan placentera.
Y tu fama por do quiera
Con gran éxito brilló;
Todo el mundo la admiró,
Y en el libro de la muerte
Por la desdichada suerte
Tu calavera se vió.

GRABADOR INTELIGENTE.

Tú serías buen grabador,
Pero toda tu destreza
No te libró de que fueras
A la tumba de cabeza.
Sacude allí la pereza
... je de ser lo que antes,
que aburrías á los marchantes,
Y ahora en tu sepulcro labra
Con buriles elegantes
En tu obsequio una palabra.

BARBERO DE BARRIO.

Muchos prodigios hiciste
Con el pelo y con la barba,
Por eso no se te escarba
La fosa en que sucumbiste.
Algunas cortadas diste
A la gente pasajera,
Mas ahora por tu tontera
Yaces dentro una mortaja,
Con tijeras y navaja
Para tuzar calaveras

DORADOR IMPERTINENTE.

A los hombres opulentos
Más de mil cuadros doraste
Y en todos muy bien quedaste
Y ellos también muy contentos.
Pero tuviste momentos
De tal torpeza y manera,
Que ninguno lo creyera
Pues hoy tienes en tus manos,
Los asquerosos gusanos
Royendo tu calavera.

FUSTERO ARRINCONADO.

A un hombre muy caporal
Famoso fuste le hiciste,
Pues por tu suerte tuviste
Una madera inmortal.
Así no quedaste mal;
Mas al dar una carrera
En su llegue pajarera
Un golpe mortal se dió,
Por eso te acompañó
A ser cual tú, calavera.

HERRERO SIN FUERZA.

A tí no te irá tan mal
Si estás en el purgatorio,
Porque es muy cierto y notorio
Que tu oficio es congenial.
En la caverna infernal,
No tendrás ningún trastorno
Revisarás en contorno
A todos tus parroquianos,
Y así echarás con tus manos
Las calaveras al horno.

El que quiera imponerse de estos esqueletos
Cinco centavos pagará completos.

THE ARTISTS'
PURGATORY
WHEREIN LIE THE
SKELETONS OF
CRAFTSMEN AND
TRADESMEN.

In this Purgatory you will find
Artists of every kind.

This picture provides palpable
proof of the principle governing all
human life and its inexorable end:
'You today and me tomorrow'.

Dozens of artists in their shrouds
Are laid out in a row.
in alphabetical order
You will find them here below.

ESTA ES DE DON QUIJOTE LA PRIMERA,
LA SIN PAR LA GIGANTE CALAVERA.

A confesarse al punto el que no quiera
En pecado volverse calavera.

Sin miedo y sin respeto ni á los reyes
Este esqueleto cumplirá sus leyes.

Aquì está de Don Quijote
la calavera valiente,
dispuesta á armar un mitote
al que se le ponga enfrente.

Ni curas ni literatos,
ni letrados ni doctores,
escaparàn los señores
de que les dé malos ratos.

THE ONE AND ONLY, NEVER TO BE FORGOT

194   LARGER THAN LIFE CALAVERA OF DON QUIXOTE

Repent your sins if you wish to save
Your soul from the torments of the grave.
Uncowed and unawed even by royalty
This skeleton will administer their justice with loyalty.

Here rides the cadaver
Of Don Quixote the knight,
Ready to take on
Any adversary in sight.

Neither doctors nor lawyers
Nor priests nor men of letters
Will escape the havoc
He wreaks on his betters.

LA CALAVERA DE CUPIDO.

También Cupido el travieso
Después de muerto es tronera,

Y llora de amor el hueso
Como todo calavera.

Fué sacerdote travieso,
Gustaba del bacalado,
Y le metía al colorado
Cuando le lloraba al hueso;
Comió también mucho queso
A solas con sus gatitas,
Tuvo sobrinas bonitas
Y aun hijas de confesión,
Fué un padrecito glotón
De muy sabrosas carnitas.

Era una preciosa güera
Que en este mundo hizo raya,
Gustó de ponerse falla,
Cupota y hasta montera;
Y sobre su calavera
Hoy luce su añeja moda;
Al andar menéase toda
Como un bergantín velero,
Y, ¡ay! vales, con ese cuero
Ni el frío, creo, nos incomoda.

También esta fué en vestir
Viciosa y usaba cola,
Llevaba sombrilla y gola
Cuando iba la misa á oir;
Le gustaba perseguir
Solteros para casarse,
Mas quiso tanto adornarse
Con chinos, que su tontera
La hizo ser sea calavera
Y á nadie puede quejarse.

Gendarme de profesión
Murió con recuerdos malos,
Resultado de los palos
Que dió con su ocupación;
Se fué con resignación
En busca de unos trompetos,
Y aquellos malos sujetos
Me lo apalearon un día
Y fué á la difuntería
A cuidar los esqueletos.

Ameme por compasión,
Pedazo de la otra vida!
—¡No me hable ya de pasión,
Calavera corrompida!

—¿Habrá perdido la fe?
—No; mi corazón espera.
—Caramba, piénselo usté.
—Pues venga, mi calavera.

—Reniego del matrimonio,
—Pues ya, maldito, qué espera
Y zás en la calavera
Dió golpes á Ñor Antonio.

Y de un sepulcro brincó
El Germán, y fué de veras,
Y con la vieja cargó
Corriendo entre calaveras.

Quien de sorbete y bastón
Camina por las aceras
Tiene en la bolsa de veras
Por lo menos un tostón;
Y es llegada la ocasión
De caminar sin tontera,
Y pedir á algún tronera
Para la copa y el sandwich,
Que todos dan en el *tianguis*
De muertos, la calavera.

De...no tiene una queja
Y pedir es importuno,
Muerte desmolada y vieja,
Calandria sin desayuno,
Tiznada olla sin oreja;
Que con sus frases sencillas
É importunas preguntillas,
Me pide su calavéra,
Espere la muy tronera
Un muerto con sus canillas.

—¡Oiga! vale no la *arrisque*
Ni beba como animal,
Y póngame un decimal
Si no quiere que lo *cisque*,
No me haga usté *misque-misque*
Con toda la trompa entera,
Pues aunque la gorda quera,
Desde luego me va á dar
Un decimal para echar
Un trago de calavera.

—Pos manaría usté salió
Dende el fondo del panteón
A buscarse su jalón
Pero aquí sí la jerró;
Con muertos no verso yo,
Ni le he de dar lo que quera;
Pues es la rata primera
Que al salir yo de mi choza,
Me pide la muy chismosa
Un *fierro* por calavera.

México —Imprenta de Antonio Vanegas Arroyo, Calle de Santa Teresa número 1.

CALAVERA OF CUPID.
Even cheeky Cupid
After death meets his due
And mourns love's passing
As will I and you.

196 Details from Calaveras.

197 CALAVERAS OF LICENTIOUS AND SAUCY SERVING WENCHES

In bars and restaurants
And ice-cream parlours,
Death nips in the bud
The serving girls' ardours.

It stalks the streets of Tacuba,
Eyeing the saloons
Where the saucy barmaids
Dispense their boons.

The plain girl's fate
Is to toil and sweat,
But the pretty wench was born
To cuddle and pet.

With their embroidered pinafores
The serving maids are
The most alluring skeletons
In the graveyard by far.

Indulgent mamas
Who accustom your daughters to leisure,
You encourage this pernicious habit
Of living for pleasure.

Of the girls who live by their wits
Today half have got
An aversion to the work
That ought to be their lot.

One has to earn one's bread
To keep death at bay,
And a barmaid gets more
Than a labourer's pay.

And the wench who becomes
A serving girl and
Plays with fire . . .
She will burn her hands.

Poor little barmaid,
What humiliation is your fare!
Poor little skeleton,
No obscenity makes you turn a hair.

And who knows what goes on
In those 'private rooms' for hire?
Not to mention the pimps
And the boors you have to admire.

But the job brings its rewards
At the end of the day.
What's the point of complaining?
Morality doesn't pay.

And these poor little skeletons
Do not deserve condemnation
Just because their parents
Were not strong on education.

Oh loving mamas,
Of your duties do not tire
Lest the flowers you have nurtured
Be sullied by the mire!

Meanwhile life goes on,
Let us enjoy the charms
Of these hired flowers
Whose fragrance disarms.

The merry serving wenches
For Duty care not a sop.
They do not want to end as skeletons
In a factory or sweatshop.

Carry on with the party,
May love and good cheer never die!
Let us be thankful that in the graveyard
Pressed tightly together we shall lie.

When we too are skeletons
(From which God us protect)
The merry serving girls
On my good advice will reflect.

There will be time later to repent
As we wait for Death's day.
In the meantime forget your sorrows
And enjoy life while you may.

CALAVERAS

ZalameraS de las CoquetaS MeseraS

La muerte por los cafes,
Neverías y restaurants,
Les va cortando los pies
A cuantas meseras hay

Por Tacuba se pasea
Mirando las picardias,
Que en muchas neverías
La mesera galantea.

Pabrecita de la fea,
Nació para trabajar,
La guapa para flirtear......
Mal haya quien no lo crea.

Son las hijas garbanceras
De mandilito bordado,
Las más chulas calaveras
Que al panteón habrán llegado.

Mamás tan consentidoras
Que a vueltras hijas mimáis
Grande contingente dáis
A esa turba que á estas horas.

Forma el cincuenta por ciento
De niñas del desparpajo;
Que le huyen al trabajo
Que debía ser su elemento.

Hay que buscar el sustento
Aunq o no sea de....calaveras
Que más ganan .as meseras
Que en la labor el jumento.

Y la niña que camina
Sobre fuego. ..sin quemarse (?)
Y que suele dedicarse
A mesera de cantina? ●

¡Oh, la pobre meserita!
Y qué do cosas aguanta...
¡Oh, pobre calaverita
Ni lo más soez le espanta!

¿Y aquellos gabinetitos
Que titulan reservados?

Que desplumar de pol itis!
Que de soportar peladoa!

Pero la chamba deja
Y se dice menos mal....
¿Que adelanta quien se queja?
¿Se come con la moral?

Además, ¿tienen la culpa
Estas pobres calaveras,
De venir de gente inculta
Que ha olvidado las escuelas?

¡Oh madres consentidoras
Que os descuidáis de tal modo!
Flores criáis a estas horas
Si pisotean por el lodo....

Entre tanto hay que vivir
Y gozar don esas flores
Cuyos prestados olores
No se pueden dilinir.

Las simpáticas meseras
Poco entienden del Deber,
Np quieren ser calaveras
De fábrica o de taller.

¡Viva la juerga, muchas,
Viva el amor, la alegría!
Alegrase en la difunteriar
No estan las fosas muy anchas.

Cuando scanos calaveras
Que Dios quiera sea muy lejos,
Recordaran mis consejca
Las simaticas meseras

Tiempo habra de pensar en esa
(buenas
Mientras llega lamuerte tan temida
Entre tanto, olvidar todas las pe
(nas
Hay que vivir y gozar de la vida.

Publicadas por la Testamentaria de A. Vanegas Arroyo. México. 5 Cets.

197

GRAN
BAILE
DE
CALAVERAS.

Llegó la gran ocasión
De divertirse deveras,
Van á hacer las calaveras
Su fiesta en el Panteón.

Las tumbas se han adornado,
Los sepulcros se han barrido,
Los féretros se han pulido
Y las lozas barnizado.

Los festejos sepulcrales,
Muchas horas durarán;
Los muertos asistirán
Con vestidos especiales.

Con gran anticipación
Calaveras y esqueletos
Se han hecho trajes completos
Que luzcan en la reunión.

México, Imprenta de Antonio Vanegas Arroyo Calle de Santa Teresa núm 1 — 1906.

CALAVERAS EN MONTON

AL PRECIO DE UN DECIMAL

Como nunca se habrá visto

EN TODA ESTA CAPITAL

Es una verdad sincera
Lo que nos dice esta frase:
Que sólo el ser que no nace
No puede ser calavera.

Esto es una ensaladilla
Para todos los mortales,
Porque hasta los militares
Les ha de dar pesadilla.

Es calavera el inglés,
Calavera, sí señor,
Calavera fué el frances
Y Faure y Sadi Carnot.
El Chino, el Americano,
El Papa y los Cardenales,
Reyes, duques, consejales
Y el jefe de la nación
En la tumba son iguales
Calaveras del montón.

Calavera el general
Y todos sus ayudantes,
Coroneles, comandantes
Y el furioso capitán.
Los subalternos serán
Calaveras en dos tiempos;
En uno son los sargentos,
Los cabos en pelotón,
Los soldados son por cientos
Calaveras del montón.

Toditos los comerciantes
Vendrán á ser calaveras
Porque ahora sí es deveras
Se acabó la Jauja de ántes,
Los cómicos resabidos
Que en todo son presumidos,
Huesos roidos y podridos
Los dueños de tendajón
Y todo dueño de giros,
Calaveras del montón.

Calavera el maromero
De cualquier circo en función,
Dueños de fonda ó mesón,
De botica ó de allí enfrente,
Todoel que engaña á la gente
Que vende todo barato;
El baratillero ingrato
Por egoista y por ahorcón
El empeñero y el beato,
Calaveras del montón.

A todos los que yo veo
Vendiendo velas de cera,
Son horribles calaveras
Que ruedan por el recreo,
Mómias secas del museo
Son toditos los neveros,
Los dulceros, pasteleros
Y fruteros en unión,
Sean también los mamoneros
Calaveras del montón.

Toditas las chimoleras
Son calaveras en mole
Y las que hacen chacualole
Juntas con las tamaleras,
Que sigan las tortilleras
Por chorreadas y liendrudas,
Las carniceras sin duda
Por vender mal chicharrón
Y el que comercia en verdura
Calaveras del montón.

MÉXICO.—IMPRENTA DE ANTONIO VANEGAS ARROYO, CALLE DE SANTA TERESA NÚM. 1.

199 Assorted Calaveras For a Modest Fee Such as Mexico City Never Did See.

201

202

200 Details from Calaveras.
201 Calavera Mourning the Dead.
202 Skeletons' Banquet.

203

203 Bloody Drama in
     Trasquillo Square.
     Murder of La
     Malagueña.
204 La Magueña.
205 Firing Squad.

Esperanza Gutierrez

(ä) "LA MALAGUEÑA"

asesinada por María Villa, después de un baile de máscaras, á las
6.20 de la mañana del lunes 8 de Marzo en la casa núm. 5 1/2 de la
plazuela de Tarasquillo.

204

BATTLES, MURDERS

205

AND ASSASSINATIONS

206

207

Batalla de Tetuán

208

206 Battle. The War in Africa.
207 The Battle of Tetuan.
208 Arab from the Riff.
209 The Great Mock Battle Outside the National Palace.

9

210

211

210 Rodolfo Gaona.
211 Ballad of Don Chepito
    Marihuano.
212 The Wrestlers. Romulus and
    Billy Clark.

212 **RÓMULUS Y BILLY CLARK.**

THE BRAGGART FROM GUADALAJARA

Bring on the pride of Guadalajara
Before he starts champing at the bit;
Unlike that Briseño of yours
Nothing will make him quit.

I'll take on anyone from Potosí,
I never yet bit the dust;
I'm from the district of Santiago,
In no second put I my trust.

If you take me for a mule-driver
Because of my shirt's fancy stitches,
You could take me for a cowboy
Because of the flares in my breeches.
Put me in front of a jaguar
And I'll not bat an eyelid;
As Tagarno here can witness
Turn tail I never did.
There's no man from Zamora
I'd not make cower in a corner.

I'm not without my charms
And I'm alwys getting hooked;
In every town and village
I have plenty on my books.
I am no backwoods boy
Nor ordinary bandit,
I'm still looking for the upstart
Who thinks he can me outwit.
On no fight would I renege
Be it with the plague.

When I visited Jalisco
I gave them a good thrashing,
In the red-light district
I cut a figure so dashing;
Manuela here can tell you
About my grooming so fine.
I came across Jesús Castro
His arms round Pancho entwined;
He called out in a huff:
Sure those pants of yours are big enough?

I have only one life
Which can be lost in a wink,
If you think you'll catch me napping
You'd better have another think.
I don't know what it means
To give in or to flag,
Even when I look beaten
My spirits never sag.
Irenea here can swear
That I ne'er did turn a hair.

You can take me or you can leave me
But Leather-Breeches here
Whatever you may say
Knows not the meaning of fear;
The man who doubts my boast
Had better say so to my face.
And if you think I ply my wares
In the market-place,
You can find others for hire
Who'll sell themselves to a buyer.

I'm the pride of Guadalajara;
From east coast to west
I've combed the nation
Putting my strength to the test.
In Colima and Tepec
I took on the most fearless,
Even in Potosí
I proved myself peerless.
I seek not friend but foe
As my big stick here does show.

EL VALIENTE DE GUADALAJARA.

Entrenle al Gualajareño
Antes que se le haga tarde;
Mire que no es un cobarde,
Y sí el mentado Briseño,

No soy como el potosino;
Ni jamás he sido arreado;
Soy del barrio de Santiago
Y no distingo padrino.

Si porque traigo pechera
Figuran que soy arriero,
Piersan que soy un ranchero
Porque porto calzonera;
Aunque vea yo á la pantera,
Nunca se me arruga el cuero
Por que no conozco el miedo;
Ya tu lo has visto, Tagarno,
Que á ninguno le recelo
Aunque fuere Zamorano.

No tengo el modo tan feo
Y me atoro en cualquier gancho;
Y por doquier que paseo,
Donde quiera lavo y plancho.
No crean que bajé del rancho,
Ni que me peleo en cuadrilla,
Vengo buscando á la *ardilla*
Por que no sabe plagiar,
Aunque es la fiebre amarilla
La contra le vengo á dar.

Por Jalisco me paseé
Y hasta les eché la pela;
Solito yo la brillé
Por el barrio "La Canela"
Ya tú lo has visto, Manuela,
Que yo nunca soy dejado;
A Jesús Castro he encontrado
Que estaba abrazando á Pancha:
Me vió y me dijo enojado:
Que no te calientas plancha?

Una vida es la que tengo,
La misma que he de dejar,
Si creen que me ando durmiendo
Todos se han de equivocar,
Jamás me sé yo aplomar,
Ni mucho menos me agüito
Aunque me vean chaparrito,
Mi alma nunca se cuartea,
Ya tu lo has visto. Irenea,
Que no le temo al prietito.

Al que no le guste el fuste
Que lo tire y monte en pelo;
Aquí está, Calzón de cuero
Y nunca crean que se asuste
Pues aquel que no le guste
Que me hable por derechito.
¿Es verdad vale bonito
Que no traigo chiquihuite?
Por hay anda el changomite
Que les trae su bocadito.

Soy tapatio muy famoso,
He andado bien la Nación,
Buscando algún fanfarrón
De los que anden por aquí,
Por Colima y por Tepic
Busqué á los de mucho tino,
Hasta el mejor potosino
Le di pruebas de hombresote;
No busco hermano ni tío,
Aquí traigo mi garrote.

214 Ponciano Diaz.

GUADALUPE BEJARANO en las bartolinas de Belen.
Careo entre la mujer verdugo y su hijo.

Las últimas noticias relativas á la *mujer verdugo*, se refieren al careo entre ésta y su hijo Aurelio, decretado por el Juez que conoce de la causa.

Hé aquí los pormenores que respecto á ese careo, da un periódico de la capital:

«En él la Bejarano se mostró más conmovida que indignada.

—Bien sé, dijo, que ésta acusación que sobre m has lanzado, hará que concluya mis días en la prisión, pero nada diré respecto de su falsedad, te perdono. Los hombres me condenarán; pero Dios que vé en el fondo de los corazones, tendrá en cuenta el sacrificio que hago de mi l.berad por que tú te salves. Que Él no te tome en cuentala calumnia que arrojas sobre tu madre.

Aurelio, pálido y abatido no contestó ni una sola palabra á los reproches de la desventurada. A las reiteradas preguntas del defensor para que negara algunos de los cargos de la Bejarano, él contestaba con el más profundo silencio.

—Quién sabe, continuó aquella, si tú serías el que golpeó á Crescencia y ahora mirando el cargo que puede resultarte, me achacas á mí tus obras.»

¡Que terrible debe ser para esa infeliz verse acusada por su propio hijo!

Ninguna esperanza le queda de poder hallar álguien que la consuele, que la vea siquiera sin horror. S is mismas compañeras de cárcel rechazaron su sociedad y se ve obligada á permanecer en tan triste encierro, sin más compañía que sus remordimientos. Quizá en esas largas noches de la prisión vea reproducirse aquellas escenas del martirio de una inocente criatura, y su imaginación le presente el yerto cadáver de Crescencia por un lado y por el otro los útiles del tormento y en el silencio de su triste encierro le parezca escuchar el llanto y los gemidos que el sufrimiento arrancaba á la desgraciada victima.

Por muy criminal y muy cruel que se suponga á una gente, no es posible llegar hasta el punto de creer que le falte siquiera un instante en que el recuerdo de su crueldad y el remordimiento de su crimen vengan á causarle un martirio atroz.

No es posible negar á esta infeliz mujer la compasión que su triste estado tiene que inspirar. La expiación, sea la que sea, no dilatará mucho en castigar su crimen. Pronto la justicia humana pronunciará su fallo.

Con una crueldad atroz
la terrible Bejarano,
ha cometido la infame
el crímen más inhumano.

A la inocente Crescencia
martiriza de tal suerte,
que esta víctima inocente
halló una temprana muerte.

La infame mujer verdugo
encuentra un grande placer
causar á esta criatura
horrible padecer.

cunda martiriza
aquellas carnes tan tiernas
con terribles quemaduras
en los brazos y en las piernas.

Años hace que otro crimen
igual á éste cometió
y por el cual la justicia
á prisión la sentenció.

Y lo que más horroriza
al pueblo que lo ha palpado,
es que de su propio hijo
su cómplice haya formado.

Y á pesar de su maldad
es digna de compasión,
por lo que debe sufrir
encerrada en su prisión.

Cuántas veces en la noche
verá su sueño turbado
por el recuerdo terrible
de aquel crímen tan nefando.

El cruel remordimiento
debe traer á su memoria
de aquellas tristes escenas
toda la pasada historia.

Y allá entre la negra sombra
de su oscuro calabozo,
de la víctima inocente
verá el espectro espantoso,

Y escuchará los gemidos
de aquel pecho acongojado,
y aquel llanto lastimero
por el tormento arrancado.

Y esta aterradora imagen
que vivirá en su delirio,
será su justa expiación,
será su eterno martirio.

Méjico.--Imprenta de Antonio Vanegas Arroyo, calle de Santa Teresa núm. 1.--Méjico.

EL JURADO

De Doña Guadalupe Martí-
nez de Bejarano y de su hijo Aurelio Bejarano, por ho-
micidio de la niña

CRESCENCIA PINEDA.

216

215 Guadalupe Bejarano in Belen Jail. Confrontation between Murderess and her Son.

216 The Trial of Dona Guadalupe Martinez from Bejarano and her son Anrelio Bejarano accused of murdering the little girl Crescencia Pineda.

217 The Crime of the Bejarano Woman.

218

1

219

220

218 Murder.
219 Ballad of the Execution of Captain Calapiz.
220 Son Kills Mother.
221 Soldiers Thrashing Women.

221

222 Details of the Latest Execution.
(This picture was used to illustrate several different executions. Vannegas Arroyo probably pulled quantities of the print in advance, leaving the rest of the sheet blank so that he could quickly set type on the 'latest' execution and get it out to the street.)

223 Execution of Luis Tapia.
224 Firing Squad.
225 Execution.
226 The Execution of Valliant.

222

223

224

225

226

LA EJEGUCION
DE VAILLANT

227

228

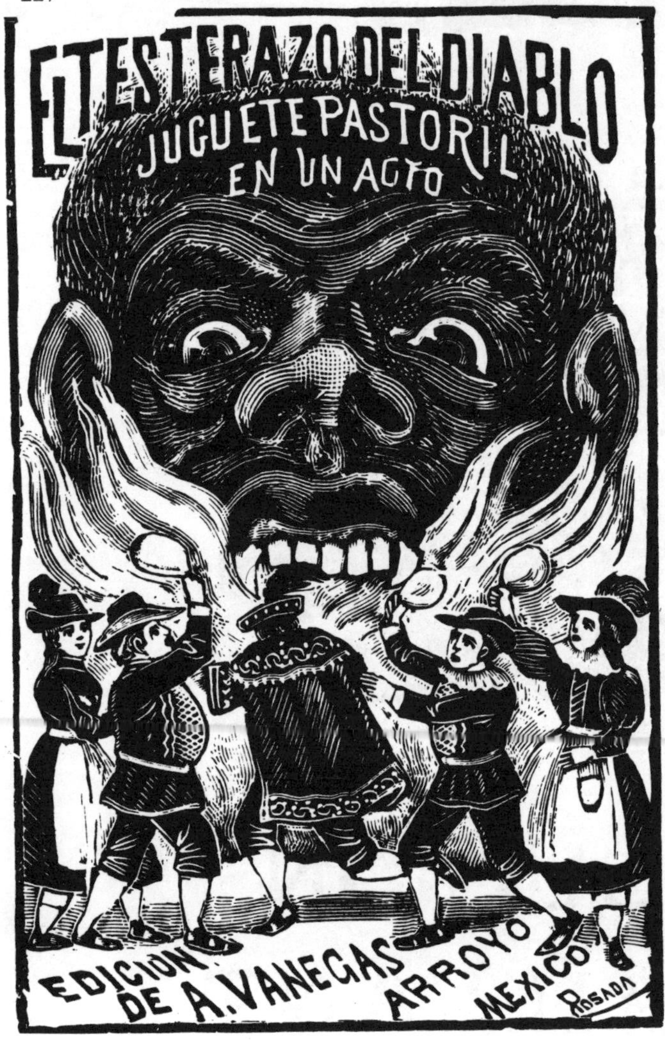

229

230

227 The Doctor. An improvised Tale.
228 The Magic Clarinet. A Story.
229 The Bump on the Devil's Head. Pastoral Skit in One Act.
230 Don Perabel. A Story.
231 Artistic Cockpit.

COMMERCIAL ART

231

232

233

232 Story of the Wolf and
the Fox.
233 Ballad of the Snail.
234 The Snake-Man

234

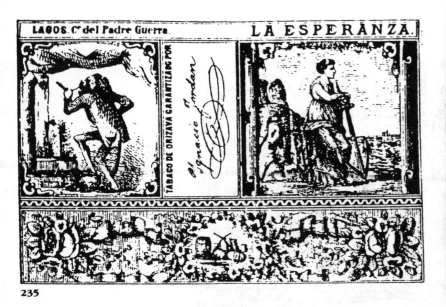

235

236

237

238

240

239

235-240 Commercial jobs produced for José Trinidad Pedroza when Posada was still an apprentice.

242

244

¡¡Lectores y Agentes de Periódicos!!

La Agencia de Encargos de David Camacho quiere hacer extensiva á toda la República la combinación de "PERIODICOS CON PREMIO" planteada en esta Capital y solicita Agentes ó suscritores directos.

243

242 Pointed Barbs.
   Column heading from *Gil Blas*.
243 Readers and Newsvendors!
   (Advertisement for the David Camacho Commercial Agency)
244 The Infernal Lantern.
   Column heading from *El Chisme*.

245 Great Triumphal Arch Erected at Number 1, Calle de Plateros, Facing the Merchants' Guild.
246 1904. The Toasts of Mexico! Porfiro Díaz and Ramón Corral Elected President and Vice-President of the Republic of Mexico by Landslide Vote.

GRAN ARCO TRIUNFAL
COLOCADO
En la 1ª Calle de Plateros
FRENTE
AL PORTAL DE MERCADERES.

RESEÑA EN VERSO
DE
LOS PRINCIPALES ARCOS
Y
CARROS ALEGORICOS
DEL
15 DE SEPTIEMBRE
DE 1899.

245

1904

¡¡GLORIAS DE MÉXICO!!

PORFIRIO DIAZ Y RAMON CORRA
ELECTOS POR EL VOTO UNANIME DEL PUEBLO
PARA PRESIDENTE Y VICE-PRESIDENTE
DE LA REPUBLICA MEXICANA.

¡Salud, oh grandes patricios!
¡Viva el Voto Popular
Que os ha sabido elevar
Por medio de sus Comicios!
   El primero de Diciembre
De mil novecientos cuatro,
Sera fecha memorable
Para el Pueblo Mexicano·
   Ese día el pueblo recorre
Las calles, con algazara
Porque Porfirio y Corral

Y por el llano de Anzures
Un comelitón regala
Para el pueblo el bravo pueb
Que vive en Paz cimentada.
   Todo en gusto y alegría
Por una elección tan amplia,
Porque Don Porfirio es gloria
De la Patria Mexicana.
   Cuando soldado en la guerr
Blandio valiente su espada
Y defendió nuestro suelo

246

EL RENEGADO

CUENTO GUERRERO

PUBLICADO POR

A. VANEGAS ARROYO.

MEXICO

247 The Renegade.
A War Story.
Published by A
Vanegas Arroyo.
(Title page)

247

248 The Green Magician.
249 A Patriot
250 Dona Caralampia
Mondongo.
251 Father Cobos.
Calendar.
252 Fater Cobos.
Calendar.

248

249

250

251

252

BOIS DE POSADA

MARIE-LOUISE. LA SUICIDÉE

Le triomphe de l'humour à l'état pur et manifeste sur le plan plastique paraît devoir être situé dans le temps très près de nous et reconnaître pour son premier artisan l'artiste mexicain Posada qui, dans d'admirables gravures sur bois de caractère populaire, nous rend sensibles tous les remous de la révolution de 1910 (les ombres de Villa et de Fierro, interrogées concurremment à ces compositions, nous renseignent sur ce que peut être le passage de l'humour de la spéculation à l'action — le Mexique, avec ses splendides jouets funèbres, s'affirmant au reste comme la terre d'élection de l'humour noir.)

André BRETON.

TÊTE DE MORT HUERTISTE

André Breton's page in *Minotaure* No. 10, 1939. The translation of the text appears on the back cover. The Calavera Huertista is more likely to be by Manuel Manilla than by Posada.

PRINTMAKER TO THE MEXICAN PEOPLE

JEAN CHARLOT

THE MEXICAN PICTORIAL RENASCENCE of the 1920s and the rebirth of Mexican fresco coincide with the rediscovery of a Mexican tradition, an adventure that proved to be fully as exciting as the making of the pictures themselves. Part of this tradition had always been in plain sight, but some of it had to be hunted down the burrows of the past and especially of the near present. The muralist claimed affinity with Mexico's public monuments which bridge a stupendous time span from archaic Totonac terra-cottas to the walls that Tres Guerras frescoed in Celaya in 1810, at the moment that Hidalgo shook the Spanish yoke from a proud neck. Just weaned from cubism, the young artist looked with loving awe at the work of those Toltec and Aztec sculptors who plied cube, pyramid, sphere, and cylinder with a taut passion beside which Cézanne's own brand of geometry retains something of the pedagogical mustiness of the classroom.

The statues and *reredos* of the Hispanic period also proved masterly models of plastic elocution for the fresco painter of the twenties groping towards a formula for public speaking in paint. He now dared, as had the colonial sculptors, to offend the rules of good taste and of plastic propriety in his urge to preach, to convert and convince. The would-be painter to the people undertook to forge a secular equivalent to the full plastic vocabulary used in the church: filigree halos, stuccoed fingers that point, bless, or damn, glass eyes bulging with ecstatis, clotted blood, flayed skins, gold damasks.

Paradoxically, the period of national independence ushered in a meagreness of taste that makes most nineteenth-century art, at least the art taught at the Academy, discussed in cultured circles, and hung in drawing rooms, little more than a provincial reflection of Europe. To the casual eye, the link with the past snaps. However, the great national tradition did not die, but went underground. Branded as folk art, a label that made it unpalatable to collector and connoisseur alike, Mexican art humbly persisted in the church *retablos* that were the people's pictures, in the *pulqueria* paintings that were the people's murals, and in the graphic works of pennysheet illustrators, rich in political and human implications.

While murals and ex-votos remain veiled in anonymity, graphic works conjure up the name of one man, Guadalupe Posada, who appears placed at the narrow neck of an hourglass where every grain of sand must pass as it slides between past and future. The bulk of an ancient and rich tradition funnelled through his work at a time when it was fated to leaven modern formulas. That Posada's stature proved equal to this task is one reason why the painters of the 1920s failed to collapse into antiquarianism as had the pre-Raphaelites and the men of Beuron.

Artists of the generation of Rivera and Orozco acknowledge their debt to Posada, although he was not a teacher and would have been mildly sceptical had anyone addressed him as "Master". In the 1890s his open studio, or rather his workshop, was tucked inside the disused carriage entrance of a private house in Santa Inez Street. Posada worked in plain sight of the passers-by, housemaids on their way to market, urchins astray from grade school, even loitering art students from the nearby San Carlos Academy. To this day Orozco, then ten years old, remembers the fat brown man in an ample white blouse, who drew and carved on metal plates with a single motion of his engraver's tools such perennial best sellers as *The Man Who Eats His Own Children, The Two-Headed Stillborn, Lovers Go to Hell on Account of a Dog, Woman Gives Birth to Four Lizards and Three Boys.* At times the shy lad would summon up enough courage to enter the workroom and purloin pocketsful of the master's metal shavings.

A little further on as he ambled to school, young Orozco passed the shop where publisher Vanegas Arroyo sold Posada-illustrated pennysheets — wholesale to city newsboys and rural peddlers — retail to houseservants and schoolboys. The plates, now become pictures, were hand tinted in sight of the customers by the women of the Arroyo clan, armed with stencils and gaudy glue pigments. One could admire in the final display such exciting subjects as "The Massacres of Chalchicomula," piles of pink corpses gashed with scarlet wounds, trampled under the *guaraches* of stretcher bearers, faces averted under yellow *petate* hats. Hero of the guerrillas against Maximilian, a maroon charro lassoed an orange gun and galloped away with his booty, leaving behind him discomfited French zouaves who blushed to match their scarlet pants. Skies remained ever serenely blue.

The bold, brusque line of Posada, all the more muscular for being dug in metal, the blatant colour patches smeared on a black and white web, made so strong an impression on Orozco that later years of studying anatomy and perspective at the art school could not uproot them from his mind or from his hand.

In contrast, the Academy of Fine Arts offered the young painter art of a far weaker character. Its halls were hung with lithographed charts of feet and eyes, clusters of ears and noses that he was enjoined to duplicate neatly in charcoal. One graduated to copying plastercasts, first in low relief, then in high relief, and lastly in the round. Relaxation was provided by a class in landscape drawing — after prints and photographs.

Such methods reached a zenith under the Catalan painter Fabres, imported by Diaz. His prideful tenure whipped Mexican artists into self-assertion at the very time when Spanish overseers were unwittingly driving Indian peons to arms.

The revolution was a Posada "still" come to life. Scenes he loved to portray — anti-

Diaz meetings with bricks and bats flying, skulls bashed in, stabbings, shootings, chained prisoners hemmed in between men on horseback — what had been but a line inked on paper found its consummation in a true depth and a true bulk. This monstrous Galatea moved in a quick staccato akin to the tempo of early newsreels, with a dubbing of deafening sound effects, pistol shots, bullet whizzes, clanking of chains, screams, sighs. Arms, till then frozen in the delicate balance of an engraved design, let fly the stones hidden in their fists. Paper machetes became steel dug into the "wicked rich," easy to spot in the cowardly uniform that Posada had devised for him, high collar and high hat, gold chain dangling on a comfortable belly soon eviscerated.

The revolutionary themes of Orozco paraphrase Posada not only because of his youthful affection for the master, but much more because the revolution was first rehearsed within this balding brown head, and its tableaux charted by this able brown hand before it had even begun. In 1922, as the scaffolds of the muralists mushroomed against the startled walls of ancient San Ildefonso, Orozco (who was far from knowing that he too would soon paint murals) smiled at the juvenile enthusiasm with which we denounced ivory towers and groomed ourselves for the role of painters to the masses. "Why paint for the people? The people make their own art." This aphorism of Orozco's, which we did not relish at the time, remains the most straightforward appraisal of Posada's function.

Posada's work falls logically into three phases, conditioned by the three mediums that he adopted in turn: lithography, wood and metal cuts, relief etching. The blandness of lithographic crayon permeates his youthful provincial manner, marks its accurate drawing and delicate half-tones. These stones are often political cartoons, big heads on spindly bodies in the taste of the French caricaturists of the 1860s. A critic ignorant of the true sequence could point to Posada's first manner as an obvious refinement and elaboration of the cruder second manner. One expects a stylistic cycle to go from simple to complex, from archaic to baroque. Posada's lithographs are valued witness to the fact that he was one of the few who consciously order their lives from complexity to simplicity.

In the coarser second manner, he cut most of the illustrations made for the plebeian tracts of publisher Antonio Vanegas Arroyo. In the meantime Posada had suffered much. The widow of Don Antonio, a charming and able matriarch who used to call me with a twinkle "El Francesito," liked to recall Posada's often-told story: How in the floods of Léon in 1887, many members of his family drowned, how they would be carried past him by the churning waters and cry "Save us, Don José," until they sank.

The role of Don Antonio in the formation of Posada's new manner was crucial. As in the middle ages when the Biblia Pauperum edified countless humble souls, so did the penny pamphlets of Arroyo in Posada's Mexico. With customers to whom reading was slow work, the picture had to state the story in terms intense enough to smoke the

Indian's penny out of his knotted kerchief. Horrifying, edifying, or comic anecdotes, broadsides on love and war, recipes for cooking and witchcraft, librettos of rustic plays, reached the remotest crags of the republic in the haversack of the peddler and the saddlebag of the pilgrim. Anthropologists who spy on remote Indian festivals and take down in phonetic shorthand the chanting, the pastoral skits, the cruel and lengthy Passion speeches, the Mystery plays that evoke a world of sharp hierarchy, man sandwiched between Heaven and Hell, might rather politely ask the coach or prompter for his book, much thumbed and yellowed, where the imprint of Vanegas Arroyo may still be deciphered.

The firm catered to the city mestizo as well as to the Indian peasant. Arroyo's *Gaceta Callejera* startled the city with extras as hot as the handsetting of type and the hand-cutting of the pictorial reportage allowed. Recurring deadlines forced Posada to cynical economies. A standard picture "doubles" for every *Horrendous Fire,* a sign on the burning house being recut each time to fit the latest and best-selling conflagration. Another print shows a street demonstration. Men shout, women scream, fists fly, banners and streamers are displayed — left blank to allow the typesetter to dub in whatever rightist or leftist slogans, whatever religious or anticlerical grievances would transform the well-worn block into the news of the day.

These uninhibited short-cuts often result in extravagant fantasies. In the first state of *The Death of General Manuel Gonzales, Ex-President of the Republic* the bearded corpse, elegantly clad in black, lies in state against a sober background of thick draperies. A few days later a second state and a new title bring the subject up to date. In *The Burial of General Manuel Gonzales, Ex-President of The Republic* a plumed hearse and high-hatted mourners, hatched out of the dark curtain, slowly cross the background of the funeral parlour with their burden and fade into its wall, watched by the corpse itself, a relict of the first state.

Each year, for the Day of the Dead, while children teased their appetites with sugar

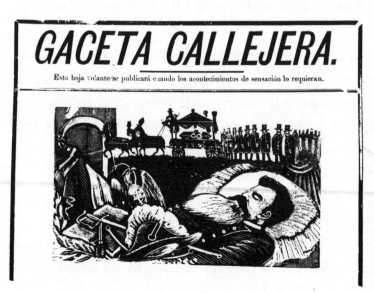

skulls and their elders prepared buffet suppers to be devoured on the family tomb, Arroyo's press let fly by the thousands broadsides known as *"calaveras,"* the Mexican Dance of Death. With high glee, Posada conjured up the skeletons of politicians with tortoiseshell glasses and celluloid collars, of generals whose ribs sag under medals, of coquettes hiding their bald skulls under the funeral flowers of imported chapeaux.

The medium of this second manner is wood, or more often, type metal. The direct cutting with burin results in a white line on black ground. While in the making, the block was coated with *azarcon.* Digging into this red lead composition helped Posada to evoke all the more easily the flames that heat and the blood that splashes his visions. The furrowed line acquires a musculation the lithographed one lacked. Journalistic deadlines, improvisations in a hard medium, and an adjustment of his plastic vocabulary to a special audience, combine to give a primitive flavour that earned for this manner the approval of Paris.

Posada's third and last manner coincides with his discovery of relief etching, made in an effort to compete cheaply with the increasingly popular process of photo-engraving. In this unusual medium, zinc is drawn upon with an acid-resisting ink, all exposed parts hollowed in an acid bath. Unlike orthodox etching, the plate is inked with a roller like a woodcut. The only other well-known relief etcher is William Blake, who claimed to have received the secret of its process in a vision from above. The result is a black line penned on white ground, and Posada, in a swagger of calligraphic arabesques, celebrates his release from the exacting bondage of the burin.

Showing no trace of naiveté, this last manner tends to irritate devotees of Posada who like to think of him as a Mexican Rousseau. Whereas the aging French master played "Clochettes" of his own composition on a three-quarter violin, we can picture the aging Mexican slapping his thigh and belching a Rabelaisian laugh as Death, his favourite model, tip-toes in.

Not all of Posada's work are prints. The widow of Don Antonio knew of two large ledgers in which the artist had sketched many scenes, "Some very nice, some very horrible," as she remembered them. A humble man, Posada did not scorn such menial tasks as came within the scope of his craft. I saw one of his circus signs still in use in the 1920s. Painted on unsized canvas and fully signed, it represented the floods of Léon with his own people drowning. This use of a personal tragedy to drum crowds under the big top is a reminder of how deeply different good neighbours may be.

It has become trite to remark that Mexican murals export badly, that they need for a frame Hispanic patios and arcades, and for lighting effects the crystalline silver of Mexico's plateau or the golden pathos of its tropics. But Mexican graphic art, uprooted, labelled, priced, caged behind glass, fares none too well either. Will the visitor to an American museum understand Posada's prints' proven function? Will he believe that the guns shoot, the blades rip, that the ink is blood?

And if he does, will he not feel cheated of an expected aesthetic delight?

POSADA'S
DANCE OF DEATH

JEAN CHARLOT

THE FOUR RELIEF PRINTS that are the reason for this essay were cut in Mexico City by José Guadalupe Posada in the very first years of this century. They are cut in metal, an alloy of zinc and lead used at the time by printers who cast and recast their own type. A genuine relic of Posada's immense *oeuvre,* they date from his mature period, after he had left his native León and come to the capital to work for Don Antonio Vanegas Arroyo. Publisher Don Antonio specialised in broadsides, street gazettes, and pennysheets. His trade was aimed exclusively at lowbrows, and cheap printing methods were essential. Nailed unceremoniously to a wood base, the metal plate was raised to type height, and both text and cut were inked and struck in one operation on a hand-operated platen press. The paper used was of cheap grade and texture, dyed in eye-catching colours, favourites being a sulphurous yellow, a shocking magenta, and a deep solferino green. To match these plebeian methods, Posada coarsened a style previously nuanced by the subtleties of lithography. In Mexico City, he forged for himself a plastic language so forceful that unequal pressures, rough stone, or gaudy hues could not weaken its impact.

Posada thought of himself as a craftsman. When at work he did not wear the smock of the artist but the green visor and large apron of the printer. Nothing in his life and work suggests that he ever felt ill at ease in his job or resentful of its ever present didactical requirements. Posada's own personal convictions fitted him easily within the narrow confines of this plebeian layout. Deadlines set by his publisher and a voracious curiosity for recording street scenes left no time even for a sigh toward far-flung aesthetic goals. Instead, Posada was ever eager to distribute his prints directly into the hands of the many, of the illiterate unwashed, of whom he was in a way the mouthpiece and for whom he lovingly evolved an alphabet of lines and values they soon learned to read fluently, though, for most of Posada's fans, the roman alphabet was to remain forever an unplumbed mystery.

For him, aesthetics never did exist in the abstract but only as the motor that moved his heavy body and kept it for hours bent double at his workbench over a tiny plate. Art was as one with the quick motions of the small-boned Indian wrist, with the deft staccato of the stubby fingers holding burin or graver. Across the street from his workshop loomed the imposing Academy of San Carlos, where art had been correctly taught since the eighteenth century. A fugitive from its classes of perspective and of anatomy, the youthful José Clemente Orozco would visit Posada at work and shyly stuff his pockets with curled metal shavings picked from the floor. For him they held, as indeed they did, some essence of the master's stocky genius.

Posada's posthumous fame threatens to enshrine his work in *catalogues raisonnés* and limit his public, outside Mexico, to curators and collectors. It is with Posada alive that I am most concerned, and how to outline his sturdy contours before they thin out in a haze of glory.

Concerning his life, its climate and habit, Arroyo's publications offer contemporaneous and articulate clues. From Don Antonio's own words — that Posada fancifully lettered in a relief etching — we learn of the publishing business that was his own as well:

> Founded in the year 1880 of the nineteenth century, this ancient firm stocks a wide choice: Collections of Greetings, Tricks, Puzzles, Games, Cookbooks, Recipes for Making Candies and Pastries, Models of Speeches, Scripts for Clowns, Patriotic Exhortations, Playlets Meant for Children or Puppets, Pleasant Tales. Also: the Novel Oracle, Rules for Telling the Cards, a New Set of Mexican Prognostications, Books of Magic, Both Brown and White, Handbook for Witches.

Posada illustrates this with a view of the Vanegas Arroyo pressroom. In what must be a self-portrait, with the familiar green visor and printer's apron, the mustachioed master hands a proof sheet just off the platen press to bearded Don Antonio, splendid in a long overcoat, high collar, and high hat. On the floor lie bundles of pennysheets ready for wholesale distribution. Idlers and passers-by hint at the street on which the workroom opened.

Another relief etching tells the sequel. We are now in the part of the shop reserved for customers. A large counter separates it from the work area where workmen in caps and aprons turn the wheels of the busy presses. Matriarch of this establishment, Mrs Vanegas Arroyo sits behind the counter, in lace collar and high hairdo, with puffed sleeves and a wasp waist. She has just sold some broadsides to a flock of news vendors.

The urchins, shoeless, coatless, straw sombreros frayed at the rim, scatter out into the street with armfuls of sheets, eager to cry their exciting wares. Two grown-up customers await their turn, one a country peddler, the other a city bureaucrat.

What these street vendors bought from Mrs Vanegas Arroyo may well have been *calaveras,* or "skulls," specifically designed for All Souls' Day. Don Antonio, and after him his son, Don Blas, and after him, his son, Don Arsacio, struck from the same blocks, year after year, "Dances of Death" brought up to date by topical allusions. In that regard the Revolution of 1910 proved a matchless boon. One day generals, bandits, and presidents were on top of the heap; the next day they were in the grave. Posada relished the epoch.

Our four pairs of skeletons are not of such exalted rank. A drunk loudly remonstrates with his loved one as she warns him of the dangers of the bottle. A policeman drags a prostitute to jail. His nightstick swings menacingly in one hand, but the other is busy pinching the fleshless buttocks of his catch. Chances are she'll swap lovemaking for an escape. The two other plates deal with a single couple. To read correctly the mind of these dead we may turn to the original broadside, dated 1906 and entitled *A Cemetery of Lovers,* that features both of our cuts, together with many another "skull." For subtitle, a ditty, probably penned by Don Antonio, is meant to whet the curiosity of the potential buyer:

Lovers lie under this sod.
Read, you who walk over it,
Of events, joyful or sad,
Stilled forever in the pit.

A street scene. A *charro,* all black leather and silver buttons, his modish pants open at the sides to reveal the flaring linen beneath. His broadbrimmed felt hat is set at a rakish angle. One fist manfully rests on the hip. He accosts a girl. She is in street costume, bell-shaped skirts, a shawl modestly hiding her bare skull. It is their first meeting. Don Antonio gives them voice:

He: Is your leaning amatory?
She: Each case depends on its merit.
He: Let's walk to the cemetery.
She: Cowboy, you talked me into it!

The next plate implies time elapsed. The two, now seated in a parlour, are in the midst of a lovers' quarrel. He half turns his back on her. Shyly she puts a hand to his shoulder:

She: Desist from such mad jealousy.
He: What! You wish me blind or one-eyed!
She: Catch a beau under my balcony,
    You may thrash him 'til he's died!

Posada's "Dance of Death" is rooted in the Gothic version that Holbein was to make his own. In Europe, Death teases, haunts, and eventually kills unthinking and unwilling humans. Posada picks up the thread of the story. Now, man and woman have crossed the momentous threshold. Their flesh has rotted away. From being the haunted, they have become haunters. Yet comedy clings to their bones more articulately than does the implied tragedy. It is its very everydayness that gives Posada's version of the hereafter its unique flavour. The Gothic "Dance" ruthlessly equated beggar with emperor. In Posada's netherworld, social niceties, and social lapses as well, are all punctiliously observed. The skeletal bourgeois walks hand in hand with his bourgeoise, with cane and umbrella displayed, along what promenades exist on their funereal planet. They give a passing nod to other genteel couples of ghosts similarly occupied. The defunct general, all bones under his plumed shako and bemedalled uniform, still brags of victories. In hellish wineshops the busy waitress is still bussed by the drunk, even though her frame has long ago spilled its stuffing.

Posada's manly art throve on revolutions, the biological one that is death and the political one that engulfed him and his beloved Mexico. Yet he remained aloof from another revolution that raged literally at his door, one that had to do with art. At the old academy next door, circa 1910, youthful students besieged and eventually roundly routed their academic teachers. The banner these hotheads rallied under was that of impressionism. It was the one revolution that sophisticates and art lovers applauded. It was the one revolution on which Posada resolutely turned his back.

b — La Calavera Infernal

De esta muerte infernal á los furore / No escaparán ni siervos ni señores,

Esta alegre calavera
Hoy invita á los mortales
Para ir á visitar
Las regiones infernales.
Habrá trenes especiales
Para recreo de este viage,
Y no habrá necesidad
De ponerse nuevo trage.

Propiedad particular.—Imprenta Santa Teresa núm. 1, y Encarnación 9.—México

---

LA HAMBRIENTA CALAVERA

Estas son calaveras — Que se pelaron deveras
Del mero año del hambre — Por flacas como un alambre

c

CALAVERA DE LA PENITENCIARIA

Primera parte.

Segunda parte

d — Imprenta de Antonio Vanegas Arroyo—2a. Calle de Santa Teresa, Número 43—México D. F. 1910

---

a Drunk Calavera.
b Infernal Calavera.
c Hungry Calavera.
d Jailhouse Calavera.

JOSÉ GUADALUPE POSADA

DIEGO RIVERA

MEXICAN ART can be divided into two quite separate tendencies, one positive and the other negative.

The former, a subproduct of colonialism, is based on the aping of foreign models to satisfy the demands of an inept bourgeoisie, whose repeated failure to establish a national economy has led to its unconditional sell-out to imperialism.

The latter, produced by the people, comprises all the rich and unspoilt cultural forms that have come to be bracketed under the term 'popular art'. Included here is the work of artists who have developed an individual style, but who have committed their life and art wholeheartedly to expressing the aspirations of the working masses. Of these, the greatest is undoubtedly the brilliant engraver José Guadalupe Posada.

Posada's inventiveness was inexhaustible, pouring out of him like a swirling torrent and putting him on a par with Goya or Callot.

According to his printer, Vanegas Arroyo, Posada produced over fifteen thousand engravings, devoted to expressing the sorrows, joys and ardent hopes of the Mexican people.

Armed with steel chisel and corrosive acid, his workman's hand carved into the metal to hurl abuse at the exploiter.

Frontliner in a guerrilla war waged with broadsheets and heroic opposition newspapers, he can be seen as a forerunner of Zapata, Flores Magón and Santanón.

He illustrated the stories, fables, songs and prayers of the common people. His satire was savage and unrelenting, yet he was a lover of life with a heart of gold. His retreat was a modest workshop in a coachyard, in full view of the passers by, next to the Church of Santa Inés and the Academia de San Carlos.

Who will erect the monument to Posada that he deserves? The workers and peasants of Mexico, who one day will bring about the triumph of the Revolution.

Posada was so great that his name may get forgotten. He is so much part of the Mexican national character that he runs the risk of becoming a pure abstraction. But his life and work infuse the spirit of the new generation of Mexican artists that has blossomed since 1923, even if they are unaware of the fact.

Entirely original, Posada's work speaks with a pure Mexican accent.

A study of his work would give a complete picture of the social life of the Mexican people.

His engravings have the essential, lasting expressive qualities that constitute true art.

Their peculiarly dynamic composition is offset by a perfectly balanced distribution of light and dark.

This blend of balance and movement is the supreme achievement of classical Mexican art, by which I mean pre-Columbian art.

Also characteristic of classical Mexican art are his love of dramatization and his macabre but at the same time humorous use of death as a plastic motif.

Posada: death personified as a skeleton that gets drunk, picks fights, sheds tears and dances for joy.

Death turned into a homely figure, into a papier-mâché puppet.

Death in the form of a candy skeleton for children to suck while their elders fight and face the firing squad, or dangle from a rope.

Death as the life and soul of the *fiesta,* dancing a fandango, or accompanying us to the cemetery to mourn the dead, and eat *mole* or drink *pulque* over their tombs.

Apart from which death is an excellent visual motif, allowing the juxtaposition of contrasting blocks of black and white, finely defined contours, bold dynamic arrangements of elongated cylindrical shapes placed at striking angles, intricate formations of bones.

In Posada's work everything and everybody is caricatured as skeleton, from the cat to the cook, from Porfirio Díaz to Zapata, including the farmer, the artisan, the dandy, not to mention the worker, the peasant and indeed the Spanish coloniser.

The Mexican bourgeoisie has been singularly unlucky in having an artist as talented and outstanding as Guadalupe Posada to chronicle and judge its manners, exploits and misadventures.

The penetrating edge of his chisel spared neither rich nor poor. In the case of the poor, he gently poked fun at their weaknesses; as for the rich, with every engraving he hurled the vitriol used to corrode the metal plate in their faces.

The patterning of light and dark, the angles and curves, the proportions, indeed everything in Posada's work is unique and masterly, ranking him among the great artists of all times.

For Posada was a classic. He never allowed himself to be governed by the sub-reality of photographic realism; he always managed to turn people and objects into plastic qualities and quantities, into constituent elements of the super-reality that is art.

If we accept August Renoir's dictum that the true work of art is 'indefinable and inimitable', we can safely say that Posada's engravings are works of art of the highest order. Posada can never be imitated; he can never be defined. In terms of technique, his work is pure plasticity; in terms of content, it is life itself: two things that cannot be imprisoned in the straitjacket of a definition.   TRANSLATED BY JO LABANYI

SELECTED BIBLIOGRAPHY

Antúnez, Francisco. PRIMICIAS LITOGRÁFICAS DEL GRABADOR JOSÉ GUADALUPE POSADA. *Aguascalientes, 1952.*

Art Institute of Chicago. POSADA: PRINTMAKER TO THE MEXICAN PEOPLE. Text by Fernando Gamboa. An exhibition lent by the Direccion General de Educacion Estetica, Mexico, *Art Institute of Chicago, 1944.*

Beals, Carleton. 'PICTURES FOR SONGS,' REVIEW OF JOSÉ GUADALUPE POSADA, MONOGRAFÍA: LAS OBRAS DE JOSÉ GUADALUPE POSADA, GRABADOR MEXICANO. ed. Frances Toor, Pablo O'Higgins and Blas Vanegas Arroyo, with an introduction by Diego Rivera. *Nation, January 21, 1931.*

Cardoz y Aragón, Luís. JOSÉ GUADALUPE POSADA. *Mexico City: Universidad Nacional Autónoma de México, 1963.*

Charlot Jean. ART FROM THE MAYANS TO DISNEY. *New York and London, Sheed and Ward, 1939.*

Charlot, Jean. AN ARTIST ON ART: COLLECTED ESSAYS OF JEAN CHARLOT. *Honolulu: University Press of Hawaii, 1972.*

Charlot, Jean. JOSÉ GUADALUPE POSADA, PRINTMAKER TO THE MEXICAN PEOPLE. *Magazine of Art 38, January 1945.*

Charlot, Jean. POSADA'S DANCE OF DEATH. *New York, Pratt Graphic Art Center, 1964.*

DAS WERK VON JOSÉ GUADALUPE POSADA. Edited and with an introduction by Hannes Jähn. *Germany: Zweitausendeins, 1976.*

Departamento de Comunicación Gráfica. EXPOSICIÓN HOMENAJE A MANUEL MANILLA, GRABADOR MEXICANO DEL SIGLO XIX. *Mexico City: Universidad Nacional Autónoma de México, 1978.*

Díaz de León, Francisco. GAHONA Y POSADA: GRABADORES MEXICANOS. *Mexico City: Fondo de Cultura Económica, 1968.*

Instituto Nacional de Bellas Artes. JOSÉ GUADALUPE POSADA: 50 ANIVERSARIO DE SU MUERTA. Text by Paul Westheim, Justino Fernández and José Julio Rodríguez. *Mexico City: Instituto Nacional de Bellas Artes/Museo de Arte Moderna, 1963.*

JOSÉ GUADALUPE POSADA (1852-1913) I WSPÓLCZESNA SZTUKA MEKSYKANSKA. Ed. Irena Jakimowicz. *Warsaw: Muzeum Narodowe w Warszawie, 1966.*

POSADA UND DIE MEXICANISCHE DRUCKGRAPHIK 1930 BIS 1960. *Nuremberg: Albrecht-Dürer-Gesellschaft, 1971.*

J G POSADA. MEXICAN POPULAR PRINTS. Ed. Julian Rothenstein. *Redstone Press, London, 1988.*

Rivera, Diego. JOSÉ GUADALUPE POSADA: THE POPULAR ARTIST. Artes de Mexico 4 *(January/February, 1958).*

Rodríguez, Antonio. POSADA, EL ARTISTA QUE RETRATÁ UNA ÉPOCA. *Mexico: Editorial Domes, 1978.*

Tinker, Edward Larocque. CORRIDOS Y CALAVERAS. *Austin: University of Texas Press, 1961.*

Toor, Frances, Paul O'Higgins and Blas Vanegas Arroyo. MONOGRAFÍA: LAS OBRAS DE JOSÉ GUADALUPE POSADA, GRABADOR MEXICANO. *Mexican Folkways, Mexico City, 1930.*

Wolfe, Bertram D. THE FABULOUS LIFE OF DIEGO RIVERA. *New York: Stein & Day Publishers, 1963.*